WHO KILLED CADE

The Silver Spurs Series: Book Three

by

Laura Hesse

Running L Productions   Vancouver Island, B.C.

Who Killed Cade

COPYRIGHT© 2021 Laura Hesse. All rights Reserved.

No part of this publication may be reproduced or transmitted in any form or by any means or stored in a database or retrieval system without prior written permission of the publisher.

The author and the publisher make no representation, express or implied, with regard to the accuracy of the information contained in this book. The material is provided for entertainment purposes and the references are intended to be supportive to the intent of the story. The author and the publisher are not responsible for any action taken based on the information provided in this book.

All characters in this publication, other than those clearly in the public domain, are fictitious and any resemblance to real persons, living or dead, is purely coincidental.

Who Killed Cade/Laura Hesse
ISBN e-book: 978-1777914301
ISBN print book: 978-1999077495

Distributed Worldwide on Amazon

Publisher: Running L Productions
Vancouver Island, British Columbia Canada
Website: www.runninglproductions.com

Cover Design by: August Sky, Selfpubbookcovers.com

Dedication

To Keddy's Bird – a Standardbred with heart

Introduction

The Silver Spurs Series is a wee bit of naughty fun meant to entertain. No harm came to any old ladies or old men in the writing of this series.

This book was inspired by Keddy's Bird, a Standardbred racehorse bought off the sulky racetrack in a claiming race. He was headed for the meat wagon, but he was in such a sorry state and so kind of eye and disposition that four girls, including me, under the age of sixteen, talked their friend and chauffeur, a thirty year-old cowboy, into claiming Keddy. Everyone needs a second chance.

Keddy was purchased and turned out on twenty-five acres with twelve other horses to run free for the winter. He never had such fun. Despite how fast the other horses galloped, Keddy never broke his pace, and got faster and faster.

He went back to racing in the spring with the cowboy driving him after applying for his racing license. Keddy was purchased for $200. His first season back he won $40,000 and top drivers were asking to race him. Keddy was sold to a racing family at the end of the season and went on to race for another five years at which time he was retired and became the family's trail horse.

Prelude

To ride a horse is to ride the wind.

The bandy-legged old man stood at the rail wearing a nondescript brown oilskin raincoat, a stained Tilley hat cocked jauntily to one side, a long silver ponytail poking out from beneath it, his icy blue eyes fixed upon the gangly dappled grey stud colt prancing by on its way to the gate. The jockey, dressed in burgundy and silver, allowed the colt named Steam Train to skip sideways towards the rail. The jockey caught the old man's eye briefly and then looked away. There was an imperceptible nod, a slight dip of the chin as the colt kicked out at the side walker's horse. The old man grinned crookedly.

Steam Train was the favourite to win, the odds only two to one, but if he placed, the odds were five to three.

Sean Finnegan, the owner and trainer of Steam Train, and his silver-blond faded trophy wife, Lacy, matched the pace of the horse along the rail. The couple strode by him, the horse's owner not even muttering an apology as he jostled the grey-haired spectator. Lacy's brown eyes glittered with mirth, her lips puckering into what she thought of as a come-hither smirk as her finger's casually brushed against the old man's before she disappeared into the crowd, her colourful rose patterned umbrella marking her progress. The pony-tailed senior would have laughed, but there was an ironic sadness to the situation that wasn't lost upon him.

Behind Steam Train walked the long shot at fifty to one. The chestnut filly's name, One Flashy Dame, didn't suit her. The filly wasn't flashy at all. She had a pencil thin neck, spindly legs, thin frame and an almost apologetic demeanour, despite being a descendant of the great Secretariat. The filly was entered into the Cup at the last minute after two scratches two days earlier. One Flashy Dame was owned by a singularly happy old lady with more money than sense.

One Flashy Dame had only run two races, floundering at the back of the pack so her true abilities were yet to be discovered. The filly had steadfastly refused the jockey's whip and urgings to run faster. She had remained like that until yesterday when her regular jockey was thrown during a training ride on another horse and broke his collar bone. A young girl with coal black hair and an infectious grin agreed to ride the filly for her elderly aunt after just receiving her jockey's license. This was going to be her first professional ride.

The old man had strolled through the stables the day before with an air of confidence, looking every bit the seasoned stock agent. No one questioned him. He stopped outside of One Flashy Dame's stall to congratulate the girl and to wish her good luck.

"Thank you," the girl grinned. "Me and Flash are going to crush it tomorrow, you wait and see. Flash doesn't like men, especially that lame brain who's been riding her."

"Is that so," the man smiled in return, turning on the charm. His blue eyes sparkled merrily as he held out his palm for the filly to sniff. 'Flash' as the girl called the filly sniffed his palm and then nuzzled his cheek, licking her lips in the process.

"Oooh, make a liar out of me, eh, girl," the jockey stuttered, her British accent kicking in.

"She's got good taste, is all," the balding horseman whispered, lovingly stroking the filly's soft velvet nose. "I rode a mare like her years ago. She'd have taken me all the way to the top if I hadn't had a falling out with the owner."

"Really," the girl said, shooting him a questioning look.

"That accent of yours, it's from Birmingham isn't it," he queried.

"It is. How did you know?" the girl grinned.

"I worked with a couple of lads from there. When I was your age all I could think of was racing," the soft-spoken horseman said, his eyes taking on a faraway look. "I was too tall for here and went to Ireland first and then England. I was thin as a reed then and willing to get on anything with four legs. Like you, it was my first professional ride. The mare's name was Star Crossed. It did her justice. She was a rangy mean tempered cow, tossed anyone foolish enough to throw a leg over her, but oh that mare could jump. It took me awhile, but finally Star Crossed and I came to an understanding."

"You were a steeplechase jockey," the girl gushed, suitably impressed.

"Aye, one of the best until I got blackballed by Star Crossed's pompous owner," the retired steeplechaser growled. "I banged about for awhile at various training stables, but the good ones wouldn't hire me, so I came home."

The tiny jockey patted his shoulder sympathetically.

"Because Flash obviously likes you and you're one of us," the girl whispered fiercely, carefully glancing around to make sure no one was within ear shot, "I'll tell you a secret."

"I don't know, luv, I don't keep secrets well," the old man replied with a shake of his head.

"Wager big on my girl tomorrow," the jockey murmured. "The weather's supposed to turn. Flash loves to run in the rain. She can take that grey in the mud any day. Also, that no talent sod who was riding her used the whip too much and she doesn't respond to that, only the voice. You got to sing to her. The faster the song, the faster she runs."

The retired jockey slapped his leg and laughed raucously. Women, they were all the same. You just needed to figure out what inspired them to get them into the winner's circle.

"I'll do that missy," he crooned to the inexperienced jockey. "You and Flash make a good team."

"Thank you," the girl beamed. "Oye, what's your name? I'll watch for you in the stands."

"O'Hara," the old man answered with a mischievous grin. "Just call me O'Hara."

"It was nice to meet you Mister O'Hara," the jockey finished, waving a goodbye to the funny balding retired jockey.

"You too, sweetie," he laughed heartily. "And you as well Flash."

The filly in the stall snorted and nuzzled him once more.

Why not, he thought to himself as he sauntered back towards the exercise yard where Steam Train's jockey was climbing aboard the grey colt, *no reason not to bet on the rookie jockey and sleepy-eyed filly. Maybe lightning would strike twice. Wouldn't that be a hoot?*

***

That was yesterday. This was today. The girl was right. The track before him was a muddy mess. The down pour that started around midnight had receded into a light drizzle, but the damage was done.

He left the rail and strode quickly through the crowd up to the long line of ticket booths inside the main building. He approached the wicket that he had been using to place his bets all day and put ten thousand cash down on One Flashy Dame to win.

"Criminy, you aren't serious," the boy at the ticket booth asked. The kid looked sixteen, not twenty-one, the peach fuzz on his chin barely passing for a beard. "You're going to blow everything you won today."

"What can I say, I love underdogs and redheads," he chortled, "and not necessarily in that order."

"Your loss," peach fuzz shrugged, handing the old man the ticket.

The retired jockey had already called his bookie to place his main bet: twenty-five thousand on Steam Train to place. His bookie had thought he was as daft as the kid did, but the girl had inspired him. Steam Train to place was a given. One Flashy Dame had a chance if the cocky young jockey was right.

The starting horn bellowed. The horses were off. O'Hara hurried back down to the gate, jostling through the crowd of raincoat clad betters until he was leaning over the rail beside the finish line.

Steam Train barrelled around the track, in the lead from the start. It was clear the grey colt was a contender for the Kentucky Derby if he continued to run like he did now. The jockey couldn't hold him back. Had O'Hara just blown thirty-five thousand?

One Flashy Dame and the cute little gal atop of her were at the back of the pack, eating mud, but halfway around the oval, the chestnut filly started to gain ground. A ray of sun peeked out from between the scuttling clouds, the light drizzle that had been falling suddenly subsiding. Waves of fog drifted along the ground making it look as if the galloping horses were painted metal pieces on a game board, their legs completely cut off by the swirling grey mist.

The retired jockey willed the filly on, revelling in the girl's expert handling of the thoroughbred. He wondered what song she was singing to the surging horse.

An opening appeared between two bays and the chestnut ploughed through it.

"And it's Locomotion in second, Everlasting Glow in third, three strides behind Steam Train. Wait! Holy cow, it's One Flashy Dame on the outside moving fast. Look at that filly run," the announcer cried.

"Come on, Flash," the old man yelled, pounding the rail with a fist, his eyes alight, his cheeks reddening as if he too was astride the filly as it barrelled past Everlasting Glow and Locomotion.

"It's Steam Train and One Flashy Dame heading for the finish line," the announcer screamed as the crowd in the stands went wild.

"It's One Flashy Dame in the lead," the announcer hollered excitedly. "Now its Steam Train by a nose, but here comes One Flashy Dame on the outside. It's One

Flashy Dame! It's One Flashy Dame! The long shot, One Flashy Dame, with rookie jockey Sadie Nesbitt on board has just won the Cup. What an upset!"

The retired steeplechase jockey hooted encouragement as the chestnut filly cantered a victory lap past the stands, soupy mud flying in every direction, the raven-haired jockey standing in the stirrups looking more like a mud wrestler than a rider, her green and gold jockey silks barely recognizable, and one hand raised in the air in triumph.

Sadie noticed the old man leaning against the rail and shot him a thumbs-up sign. He tipped his hat to her in a silent salute.

Behind One Flashy Dame cantered the former favourite, Steam Train. The jockey shook his head in mock consternation as he rode the mud splattered grey stud colt past some very angry betters.

O'Hara followed the crowd to the winner's circle, unable to suppress his joy. One Flashy Dame and her diminutive jockey together had just won him a half million bucks.

He was delighted to see the filly's owner, aided by a racetrack employee, hobble into the winner's circle to receive an armful of red roses from the racetrack manager. The old woman reminded him of Queen Elizabeth so regal was her stance and wave to the crowd of onlookers, the bouquet of roses almost as tall as she was.

"You idiot," Sean Finnegan shouted at his jockey. "How the Hell could you lose to that fleabag? And to a rookie jockey?"

The crowd booed loudly as the grey colt spooked sideways away from the furious trainer.

"Just wasn't our day, boss," the old man heard the jockey say. "Train's not a mudder."

One of the course administrators raced to the scene, hauling Finnegan to one side to caution him. Lacy Finnegan, ever the lady, took a moment to speak a few words of encouragement to Sadie and her over-the-moon happy auntie, ignoring the furious glances of her husband.

O'Hara would have laughed, but the smile was wiped from his face when the jockey aboard Steam Train shot him a pointed look.

Really, the old man grimaced. *You think you're going to get paid when One Flashy Dame clearly won the race by sheer talent?*

The old man whistled happily as he walked up to his favourite ticket window.

The kid behind the window shot him a high-five through the Plexiglas.

"Man, you sure called it. I got to wait for the manager for this though," peach fuzz grinned. "The track manager will want a picture with you and your winnings cheque, I'm sure."

"No pictures," the pony tailed punter responded, his visage clouding over.

"Okay, but I still need your name for the cheque," the kid wheedled.

"Make it out to… Cade O'Hara," the old man grinned, his trepidation fading. "That's C.A.D.E. Cade with a 'C', and O. Apostrophe. H. A. R. A. O'Hara."

"I can spell, you know," peach fuzz grumbled.

Chapter One

Life without you would be a pointless pencil.

"I think it's going to be a hot one today," the pretty forest ranger crooned in Gus' ear, snuggling up beside him as he finished washing the last of the breakfast dishes.

They had made a deal: the cook didn't have to clean. Dee's breakfast of scrambled eggs, sausages, bacon, fried ham and flapjacks would last him until supper time. It was only fair he clean-up after the class five hurricane named Gallant swept through the kitchen. Even then, Gus figured he got the better end of the deal.

"Let's ride up to the lake before it gets too hot," Gus suggested, drying his hands on a dish towel.

He swivelled around, reaching out to the woman curled around him like a python and swept a lock of dark hair from her upturned face.

"And what kind of trouble should we get into at the lake," she grinned, her brown eyes sparkling with mischief. "Something naughty, I hope."

"I can think of a few things," the handsome ATF agent whispered into her luscious hair, the soft scent of her coconut shampoo tickling his nostrils.

"I'll go saddle the horses," the ranger laughed, pulling away.

"You do that," he grinned.

Dee swatted him playfully on the behind before exiting the house.

Gus watched his girlfriend sashay across the yard towards the barn, her arthritic Border collie walking slowly behind her. The dog didn't come on trail rides anymore, too crippled with age to endure the miles of rough terrain. They had almost adopted one of the Montana's Saint Bernard puppies last year, but it wouldn't have been fair to the collie.

Sometimes, Gus's love for the sensuous forest ranger overwhelmed him... like now, his pulse was beating so fast, he thought his heart was going to explode out of his chest like the creature in the movie 'Alien'. When he wasn't with Dee, he longed for her. Gus wanted to be with her every moment of every day, now and forever, protecting her, loving her. He wanted to know that when he came home, she would be there.

Gus sighed. He had never had a real home, only one foster home after the other growing up until he joined the marines, but now this small acreage in the middle of nowhere felt like the place he belonged.

He had seven days left to put his plan into motion. Fingers crossed; it would go without a hitch.

Outside the house, Dee grabbed a couple of halters and walked across the pasture towards the bay mustang and Quarter horse grazing in the field. The horses whinnied as they greeted her.

The mountains in the distance looked like a watercolor painting, the multilayered shades of green, grey and brown muted by the early morning heat haze. The sky was pale blue. Traces of long white clouds hovered above the mountain tops. The fields in the valley were mostly brown, the last of the season's hay already cut and drying in the sun.

The hardened Afghanistan vet's strong jaw line and brown eyes softened as he observed the scene with childlike wonder.

Gus pulled his cell phone out of his back pocket and dialled his sister. She was an early riser.

"Yo, bro," his sister laughed, picking up the call on the second ring. "I'm just heading down to breakfast. Good timing. What's up?"

"I need your help," Gus chuckled, imagining the redheaded minister pushing the glasses up her nose as she talked, a habit she had since childhood.

"Do I need to wear my vestments?" asked the smooth silky voice.

"No," he chuckled. "I'm planning on asking Dee to marry me and I want it to be special."

"Ahh, now even I'm blushing," his sister replied.

"You know how I told you she's always rescuing wounded animals," Gus grinned. "Well, I had this idea to send her out looking for a wounded owl or eagle or something like that, but instead of finding the bird, she'd find me with a ring and a bunch of flowers."

There was a pause at the end of the line followed by a hearty laugh.

"Bro, I never knew you were such a romantic," was the startled reply. "I'm in. I can't wait to meet the woman who has turned my brother into mush. I would suggest that 'a bunch of flowers' bears thinking about."

"Okay, okay, maybe roses. Heck, I don't know if she even likes them," Gus said, exasperated. Leave it to his sister to want to know every detail. She was always like that.

"Chill, man, I just want to help. Once she finds you instead of a bird of prey, not that you don't fit into that category, exactly what are you going to say?"

"I dunno, maybe say something like 'life without you is like a pointless pencil, and now it's not pointless anymore," Gus answered, not having given that part much thought.

"Yeah, maybe work on that a little," the pastor laughed. "I suggest you stay with the basics, you know, a stupidly expensive gigantic diamond ring followed by a 'will you marry me?'"

"Dee's not the type to want a gigantic ring. It would make it hard to bridle a horse, might poke an eye out, but I hear you, sis. When can you be here?"

"In a few days," she replied. "The retreat is over tomorrow. I have an interview with the archbishop today about a posting he can't fill, plus I've got a eulogy to perform for a couple of biker friends and then I'm all yours."

"Sounds good. Take care and I'll see you soon," he grinned.

"Will do."

Gus ended the call. The one good thing that came out of his scattered upbringing was his sister. Once they met, two kids alone in the foster system, they vowed never to leave each other. They had kept that vow, but he hadn't seen her in three years. Gus couldn't wait for Terri and Dee to meet.

The rest was pure planning. How hard could it be? Right? Emma and Sam Montana were his next recruits. They could help him finalize his engagement plans. Funny, him asking Emma for help. He had promised Cleve,

Emma's husband that he would look after her if Cleve didn't make it back from Afghanistan. Gus had been attracted to his best friend's widow at first and wanted to fulfill his promise to her husband, but Emma was already smitten. Sheriff Cole Trane was the focus of her desire.

The moment Gus laid eyes on the ranger riding up the canyon, a wanted felon on her horse, he was hooked. She was something out of a Conan the Barbarian novel, both beautiful and wild. Life without Dee was too horrible to contemplate.

"I'm not saddling your horse for you," Dee yelled from the barn breaking into his reverie.

"Coming," Gus hollered in return, stuffing his cell phone back in his rear pocket.

Life was good, he mused as he sauntered out of the house towards his soon-to-be fiancée, the screen door banging shut behind him. *Yep, life was good indeed and he was pretty sure Dee would say 'yes'.*

***

"I think we should all go for a ride after breakfast," Mary said, using her fork as a pointer stick. "The horses could use an outing and so could we."

"Oh, I don't know," Zoe replied diffidently, pushing an unruly strand of grey hair out of her face. "I need to go into town and get a trim."

"Yes, you look like Harry Potter," Sylvie joked.

"I do not," Zoe grumbled. "My hair isn't even black anymore. Wait, do you think I should dye it?"

"I'm just pulling your leg," Sylvie laughed.

"You can get your hair done any time," Mary argued.

"Mary's right, we should go for a ride," Sylvie agreed. "It will be too hot later on to do anything but nap or preen ourselves, preferably in some place with air conditioning."

Sylvie's compatriot, Mary Adams, a Dolly Parton look-alike, glanced her way. The pair exchanged a grin. Laugh lines creased the corners of Mary's blue eyes.

Sylvie smirked as she looked around the table at the fellow residents of The Silver Spurs Home for Aging Cowgirls. After five years in a wheelchair thanks to a massive stroke, the move to the Montana ranch, the subsequent death of her cheating husband, the disappearance of his body, and her kidnapping by two bumbling bandits, a peaceful morning ride was just the ticket to kick off the day.

Zoe rolled her brown eyes.

Ever since Zoe and Maggie had ventured into Mexico to retrieve three million dollars of ransom money to free her and Mary from the kidnappers, Zoe's ten minutes of fame on national TV had made Zoe more than a little overbearing. Zoe's ego had swelled to monstrous proportions.

"What do you think, Butch," Zoe queried the black-haired sultry woman of Spanish Cherokee Irish origins sitting to the left of her.

"Don't call me that," Maggie snapped. "And stop insisting I call you Sundance. It's annoying."

Maggie Carroll was still beautiful at seventy-three years-old, but she had soured since she had stopped visiting the notorious smuggler Tommy Cortez in prison. Not that she'd been a happy person to begin with, Sylvie mused, but Maggie's depression was sucking the life out of her and everyone else at the table.

Zoe and Maggie had been bitter rivals for a time. Now, they did everything together, albeit with a feline cattiness that would make a preacher blush. They had terrorized the blackjack dealers in Vegas after the kidnapping fiasco. Mary and Sylvie had joined them once the doctors had given them the okay. Those were good times. It felt like eons ago.

"I suppose Storm could use an adventure," Maggie mumbled into her coffee cup. "He has been a bit uppity lately."

"Mags, Storm is always uppity," Sylvie chortled.

"I guess Zippo could use some down time too," Zoe finally agreed. "BJ's done a marvelous job with him, but a day out of the ring would do him good."

'It's settled then," Mary laughed lightly, clapping her hands together. "We'll take the stallions out."

"What's settled," Sam Montana asked, striding into the room. He made a beeline for the coffee pot, his cowboy boots clumping across the hardwood floors, his sweat stained Stetson tipped back on his head, his white moustache twitching as he eyed the ladies suspiciously.

Sylvie felt her pulse quicken. Sam Montana cut a striking figure with his tanned face, hazel eyes, and salt and pepper hair. He gazed down upon her, his head tilting slightly sideways. The look he gave her made her heart flutter.

Part of Sylvie wished desperately that they could find Cade's body and get it over with. She had confessed to killing him, but then Cade up and walked right out of the outhouse where she had placed him. Cade always was contrary though, so it wasn't a complete surprise.

Still, a body would be helpful. If Zoe and Maggie could have conjugal visits with a felon, then surely Sylvie could arrange for conjugal visits with Sam. Sam was such a God-fearing man; the only way their unspoken love would ever be shared was if Cade turned up, dead or alive.

"We're going for a trail ride," Sylvie grinned, eyes fixed upon Sam. "The studs need a little time in the saddle."

"They do, do they?" Sam chuckled.

"They aren't the only ones," Mary muttered into her teacup.

Sam and Sylvie smothered a laugh.

"Do you think Emma will be home soon," Zoe queried. "Maybe she'd like to come with us?"

"Nice thought, but don't count on her," Sam said, refilling his coffee mug. "She's picking up groceries and has some other errands to run after she drops the kids off at their friends' houses."

"Well, then we may as well run upstairs and change into our breeches," Maggie declared, pushing away from the table.

"Indeed," Zoe agreed, daintily dabbing her mouth with a napkin.

"While you two get all dolled up for your stallions, Sylvie and I will clear the table," Mary chastised the pair.

"You don't have to," Sam grumbled. "Emma will clean the kitchen when she gets back. That's what you're paying us for."

"Sam Montana, I think we are more than capable of putting our own dirty dishes into the dishwasher and wiping down the kitchen counters for Emma," Sylvie quipped.

"Yes, ma'am," Sam stammered, raising his hands into the air in supplication.

"You two need to get a room and get it over with," Mary laughed, wagging a finger at Sylvie and Sam. "And don't go looking at me like that, Sam. I've known you way too long. It's about time you got off that high horse of yours."

Sam guffawed, blushing from head to toe. Sylvie fought the urge to throw herself across the kitchen table at him. He looked so darn adorable.

Maggie glowered. Zoe laughed delightedly, having given up long ago on convincing Sam to be husband number seven.

"I'll go water the stallions before you go," Sam harrumphed, performing a quick about face and racing out of the room as Maggie and Zoe marched out of the kitchen behind him.

"Well, that's one way to clear a room," Sylvie joked to Mary.

She and Mary burst out laughing.

Chapter Two

One man's wrong lead is another man's counter-canter.
S.D. Price

Johnny Brillio sat in his office overlooking the dance floor and bar. The cleaners were busily cleaning up party streamers and unplugging the toilets after a wild bachelor's party the night before. Two of his men sat quietly at the bar drinking coffee watching the women work.

The night club rocked from ten o'clock at night to one in the morning, the Puerto Rican DJ he had hired rocketing his club to fame in less than three months. The kid had talent according to the hotties who lined up every Thursday, Friday and Saturday nights to see him flex his muscles and shake his bootie along with them. The club was never supposed to make money, but, hey, "never look a gift horse in the mouth," Johnny's old man used to say.

His stomach grumbled, bile rising into his throat as the bar's double front doors opened and in walked the bowlegged pony-tailed geezer he had been waiting for all morning. There was a spring in his step, the old boy appearing to not have a care in the world. Johnny grimaced, he probably didn't.

Six months ago, O'Hara had come into the club a broken man with bent shoulders, sallow skin, and a shuffling gate. Today his skin glowed with good health, his back was straight, and a smile creased his lips.

Must be getting laid, Johnny thought. *Lucky him.*

Johnny popped a couple of cherry flavoured Tums into his mouth.

He saw O'Hara look up at him through the Plexiglas office window. Johnny's men held him at bay. No one got past his cousins. It helped that they were family and had a stake in the operation.

Johnny sighed and swivelled in his chair, popping open the safe. It pained him to take out the large stack of one-hundred-dollar bills O'Hara had won on yesterday's race: twenty-one thousand in total. He liked it better when the rubes lost. At least he still had a stake in the game. The chinks were undercutting him left and right and the Cartel was talking about branching out too. Everyone wanted in on the action these days. He didn't want to even think about all the Russian online gaming sites.

The middle-aged dark-haired olive-skinned night club owner and bookie to the down-and-out waved to his men. Immediately they stood aside and let the daily jackpot winner up the stairs to collect his winnings.

"Top of the day," O'Hara said as he approached the bookie.

"O'Hara," Johnny nodded, sliding the cash across the table to the dapper gambler. "You get a hot tip or something?"

"You could say that," the old man grinned.

Johnny snorted in amusement.

"This feels a little light," O'Hara hissed, thumbing through the bills.

"It is. You had a tab, remember," Johnny snapped, his eyes narrowing. *Who did this bozo think he was?* If it wasn't for the fact that O'Hara had the luck of the Irish and won on a semi-regular basis, Johnny would have never fronted him the bet in the first place.

"You owed me ten thousand plus interest which made it fifteen thousand. You think I'm gonna let you walk out with the whole kit and caboodle?"

O'Hara glowered and pocketed his winnings.

"I need a favour," O'Hara said, taking a seat across from Brillio without asking.

"And that is," Brillio replied gruffly.

"I have a cheque that needs cashing," O'Hara responded, leaning across the desk. "It's a rather large one. I expect you'll need time to put the funds together."

"You win the lottery or something?"

"Or something," the old man shrugged. "It's all legal, I can assure you. I bet on a mudder to win the cup. The track was a bog. Damned if the filly didn't come through."

O'Hara pulled the racetrack cheque from his wallet and slid it across the table.

"I know. The long shot beat the favourite. I made a bundle on that race," Brillio chuckled, sliding the cheque the rest of the way forward.

"Jumping Jiminy," the bookie hissed, his eyes widening at the number on the face of the rectangle of paper. "Five hundred big ones, are you kidding me?"

"Not at all," O'Hara laughed.

Johnny was speechless. That didn't happen very often.

"Why not go to a bank," he queried, confused. "I mean, it looks legit and I watched the race. It was all over the news."

What was the problem here?

"I'd rather not go to a bank," the old man wheedled. "I don't want questions and I definitely don't want any more publicity than the track has already released. It was hard enough skipping out without a hundred photos being taken of me. The ruddy news crews were everywhere."

"I expect they were," Johnny muttered.

"Of course, I expect to pay a healthy percentage for the service," the retired steeplechaser chimed.

"Fifty percent," Johnny demanded. "I can't put it through my business, or it'll trigger a tax review. I got to go outside and that means more grease on the wheels."

"Fifty percent is highway robbery," the old man shouted, spittle flying.

"Take it or leave it," Johnny smirked.

"Thirty percent," O'Hara countered.

"Forty."

"Thirty or nothing."

"Done," Johnny agreed. He could do that. Thirty percent of five hundred thousand was nothing to sneeze at. "Give me a couple of days."

O'Hara stood up to leave.

"One day you're going to have to tell me how you pulled it off," Brillio said, sizing up the gambler. "It had to be rigged. Not that I'm complaining, mind you. Most of the action was on Steam Train to win."

While the Tilley hat had seen better days, the old man's button down green and blue plaid shirt, designer jeans, and brown leather cowboy boots were all brand spanking new.

"What can I say, the horses love me," he purred, eyes a light with mischief, "and so do the ladies. I can assure you that the win was righteous."

For a moment, the years rolled off the aging gambler and Johnny caught a glimpse of the impish young man O'Hara used to be beneath the weathered exterior.

Johnny reached across the desk and shook the gambler's hand. His handshake was firm and strong.

The old man nodded and then left.

Brillio walked across the room to the mini bar. He poured himself a shot of Scotch and returned to his desk. The white cheque with the racetrack's green logo, the name Cade O'Hara typed neatly across the face, and the sum of five hundred thousand dollars printed in capitals was as crisp as an autumn morning. He placed the glass of Scotch on the table beside the cheque and sat back down.

It was funny; he never knew the rube's first name. All bets were cash. He had no doubt the cheque was real, but he would call the racetrack to make sure Cade O'Hara wasn't conning him and somebody else was the winner of record. Nothing surprised Brillio anymore, not in his line of work.

"Lucky schmuck," he mumbled.

***

O'Hara stood outside the After Eight Night Club letting his eyes adjust to the bright sunlight. The fifteen thousand was burning a hole in his pocket.

"First things first," he grinned.

He owed people, bad people, but he didn't care. A T-bone steak dinner, a bottle of Jack Daniels, and a quick phone call to Lacy to see if she could slip away to Vegas for a little bump and grind was at the top of the agenda.

He lifted a hand and hailed the yellow cab rolling by the club. His luck had turned. Life was good.

The cab screeched to a halt and backed up to the curb. O'Hara opened the back door.

"The Dominion," he said to the cab driver as he climbed in.

"I don't do the east end," the cabbie growled. "Find someone else."

"You do now," O'Hara barked, waving a hundred-dollar bill in front of the cabby's face. "I'll only be a few minutes, and then we'll head over to the Hilton."

"Whatever you say, Mister," the cabbie smiled snatching the bill out of O'Hara's fingers.

O'Hara leaned back in the seat.

Maybe he should hire a hooker instead of calling Lacy? Lacy was getting a little long in the tooth for his liking and he had more than enough money to hire a clean and seasoned pro. The image of Julia Roberts in Pretty Woman filled his mind. He loved that movie. Yep, a long-legged brunette was in order. Redheads and bleached blonds were a thing of the past.

Still, he supposed, his conscience nagging at him, he owed it to Lacy to see her one more time before flying off to Reno and cutting her out of his life forever.

Chapter Three

What the colt learns in youth he continues in old age.
French Proverb

Water droplets beaded the sides of the canvas tepee. Steam billowed out the opening at the top of the tent. Inside the tepee Retired Marine Corp. Pastor Terri Scallon and Reverend Elizabeth Smyth, an Anglican minister, sat cross-legged in front of a pile of rough pale green olivine and slick black vulcanite rocks.

"More," Elizabeth asked, holding a metal ladle of water over the mound of rocks. Elizabeth's eyes glittered with determination; her mouth set in a thin line.

"Bring it on, sister," Terri grinned, her face the colour of an over ripe watermelon.

Elizabeth poured the water over the rocks. The water sizzled. Blistering hot steam billowed upwards.

Terri swayed like cattails in the wind. Her vision blurred. Rivers of sweat rolled down her face and into her eyes. Terri swore she felt the blood in her veins bubbling. Her one consolation was the silver-haired woman sitting beside her was in as much discomfort as she was, if not more given her age.

Terri closed her eyes, a wave of dizziness sweeping over her. The blistering, fetid air inside the tent was rank. It smelled of unwashed bodies and oiled canvas. Nausea threatened to overwhelm her, but she refused to give in. The gauntlet had been thrown. The indomitable Reverend Smyth had insinuated over a simple breakfast of porridge and blueberries that women ministers didn't belong on the front lines, that they weren't strong enough to handle the 'heat' so to speak. Terri hadn't expected that comment from another woman and was determined to prove Reverend Smyth wrong.

"Right, ladies, lunch is being served," a husky male voice said from outside the tepee. "You've proved your point."

"Oh, praise the Lord," Elizabeth huffed, rolling sideways to uncurl her legs. "I was only kidding you know."

"You were what?" Terri boomed.

"You army types take things so seriously," the older woman grumbled as she grabbed hold of a tent pole and pulled herself to her feet.

The red-faced buxom senior offered Terri a hand.

Terri laughed as she accepted the reverend's hand and rose shakily to her feet. For a minute she thought she was going to fall face first into the rocks, but two hands shot out and steadied her.

"Last one in is a rotten egg," Elizabeth grinned before racing buck naked out of the tepee, boobs and butt cheeks flapping.

"Oh, no you don't," Terri shouted, barrelling out of the tent like a drunken sailor.

With a resounding war-cry, the flaming haired pastor raced across the grass, past the shocked archbishop, the

Anglican minister, and several other retreat participants on the way to the dining hall for lunch. She dove into the crystal-clear lake and came up shrieking as the bite of the icy water hit her lobster-coloured skin.

Reverend Smyth dove in after Terri, swam a short distance under water, and then rose out of the lake like a nymph, albeit a sixty-year-old one.

"Well now that's something you don't see everyday," the archbishop crowed.

Terri sputtered, her skin basking in the cold chill as relief flooded through her pores.

"I must say," the round-eyed archbishop joked, "that if ever I have a chance to listen to one of your sermons and find it boring, I can always picture you both naked."

The archbishop laughed heartily before heading up the hill to the lodge.

Terri glanced sideways at Elizabeth.

"Don't worry, dear, a Catholic archbishop is highly unlikely to come to an Anglican minister's sermon, let alone an army pastor's one," Elizabeth offered. "It's amazing that he's at this retreat at all. Catholic clergy are generally a stuffy lot."

"Marines, not army," Terri murmured.

"Really, Terri, you must stop taking things so seriously," the old woman chided her.

"True, but I have an interview with him later on," Terri confided.

The Reverend Elizabeth Smyth started to laugh, a great big belly laugh that echoed through the woods and across the lake. Terri couldn't help but follow suit.

Together, the two ordained ministers walked out of the lake and across the lawn to the tepee where their robes hung on pegs outside of the door.

"So, you aren't enlisting for another tour then," the older minister asked.

"No, I'm considering a posting to an ink spot of a town in the mountains," Terri replied. "The town's minister passed away two years ago, and they haven't been able to find anyone willing to go there; hence, my interview with the archbishop. The church falls under his purview. My last tour was brutal. I thought some time in the mountains would do me good. In the meantime, I have a funeral to preside over and perhaps a wedding to perform."

"Oooh, how lovely, do tell me more," Elizabeth purred.

***

While Terri was cooling her fiery skin, her stepbrother was stoking the flames of love while half-submerged in a glacial lake, his arms wrapped around the voluptuous body of the forest ranger that had captured his heart.

The couple's two horses, a bay Quarter horse and mustang, grazed alongside the azure water, tails flicking away the angry horseflies that nipped at their sweaty bellies. Two mounds of clothes rested neatly atop the Western saddles tipped sideways against a rocky outcrop some distance away. A hawk circled lazily in the hazy summer sky, its shadow flitting across the tranquil scene below.

"I can't believe it! No emergency calls. No drug dealers to arrest. No illicit guns to seize. No mountain lions to track down. Whatever will we do to keep ourselves busy?" Dee crooned.

"Shhh, you'll jinx us," Gus chuckled.

"Heaven forbid," Dee grinned, the skin around her dark brown eyes crinkling with mirth.

Gus kissed her, his tongue darting between her lips, his heart beating furiously. Dee responded with equal need and passion.

A soft woof and a loud splash startled them.

The couple spun around.

A monstrous fluffy sable and white Saint Bernard, still a puppy at a hundred and ten pounds, jowls trailing in the water, eyes bright, swam happily towards them.

"Junior, what are you doing here," Dee sputtered.

"I bet she's not alone," Gus cried in alarm, scanning the shore for Junior's mother.

Almost immediately, Bulldozer Senior, Junior's mother, galloped up the winding lake trail. She stopped at the shore to check out what kind of trouble her offspring had gotten into.

Bulldozer, aka Dozer, had another thirty pounds on her son, but Junior wasn't finished growing yet. Her coat was silkier than the pups, darker brown and black intermixed with the sable. She splashed into the water and then lay down in the shallows.

"What? Don't tell me you can't swim," Gus teased the dog.

Dozer swirled sideways, sending spirals of waves circling outwards, seemingly fascinated by her tail's elegant motions in the water.

"I hope the kids aren't with them," Dee moaned, ruffling Junior's head as he swam past.

"Speaking of that," Gus added, nervously scanning the trail. Dee blushed and lowered herself deeper into the water until only the tips of her shoulders were showing.

"Don't let us disturb you," Mary called innocently from atop her brown and white blue-eyed paint stallion.

"Definitely, do continue," Sylvie chortled, reining her gigantic, dappled bay Hanoverian stallion in beside her friend's. The Hanoverian towered over the paint horse. The two stallions were so low key and well behaved under saddle that they didn't bat an ear at the others presence.

"What's going on," Zoe called, prancing into the clearing on her elegant white Andalusian stallion. The stallion snorted and sidestepped away from the other two studs, leaving room for Maggie astride the temperamental chestnut Trakehner.

The chestnut pinned his ears back and danced on the spot, the raven-haired bronzed skin rider on top of him unruffled by the horse's antics.

Gus and Dee's horses looked up from their grazing. The mustang whinnied shrilly and snorted a warning.

Gus was relieved that Dee had insisted on hobbling their horses.

"Sex in the wilderness, how uncouth," Maggie grimaced.

"Oh, Mags, where's your spirit of adventure," Sylvie laughed lightly.

"I think it's marvellous," Zoe giggled. "Mervin and I made love in the naughtiest of places."

"Not now, Zoe," Maggie grumbled, rolling her eyes heavenward.

"What's wrong with sex on an elevator," Zoe asked innocently. "And believe me; becoming a member of the Mile High Club is no easy feat. I mean, have you seen the size of those airplane bathrooms?"

"I for one want to hear more," Mary replied.

"Let's not," Gus growled.

"Oh, I don't know," Dee whispered hoarsely, "I'm sure we could learn a thing or two from Zoe. How many husbands have you had? Five?"

"Six," Zoe sighed.

"Ignore us," Mary beamed. "Continue with what you were doing. We'll just water our horses and be off."

"Right," Gus groaned, his eyes narrowing as he saw Sylvie and Mary exchange a knowing look. He was never going to hear the end of this. He had planned on stopping at the ranch later to talk to Emma and Sam about helping him plan his crazy marriage proposal, but he wasn't so sure about that now. Maybe he should keep it simple.

"Come on, Junior, let's leave these two love birds to their own devices," Sylvie grinned, motioning for the pup to join her.

The dog swam back to shore. He emerged from the lake dripping wet and shook himself off. Water droplets flew in every direction. The stallions skipped sideways. Maggie's stud leapt into the air like a ballerina on steroids.

Bulldozer lifted her bulk out of the lake, snuffled the pup, and then satisfied that everything was in order, wandered over to a bush and squatted, lake water mingling with urine in the dirt below her.

Maggie settled her stallion as the other three loosened their reins and let their horse's drink. A superior, if not haughty look was affixed to Maggie's face.

Typical Maggie, Gus grinned in amusement. It was the other gals he worried about. They were up to something, he could tell. The Mona Lisa grins didn't fool him. The wheels were turning.

Under the water, Gus reached for Dee's hand. Her strong fingers curled around his. He glanced sideways at Dee wondering is she was sensing anything untoward from the ladies as they sat peacefully in the saddle, looking anywhere but at the naked couple in the lake. Dee raised an eyebrow in response, completely unruffled.

"Look at this way," Dee whispered in his ear. "At least these cougars don't have fangs and claws."

"Want to bet," he whispered back.

"Right-o, we're off," Zoe cried cheerily as she backed up her stallion.

"Don't forget the sunscreen," Mary advised, spinning the paint on its haunches. "Believe me, there are places better not to get burnt."

"You know we could leave the dogs with you for security if you want," Sylvie offered as she waited for Maggie to move the wild-eyed chestnut aside.

"NO!" Gus and Dee yelled in unison.

The ladies, including Maggie, giggled as they rode off.

"Now, where were we," Gus said, nuzzling Dee's neck as the twang of horseshoes on gravel faded into the distance.

"I think we were here," Dee crooned, sidling up against him.

Gus pulled her close, spinning Dee around in a tight embrace. He was just starting to relax when muffled laughter flitted towards them. It sounded like children in a funhouse. Sylvie and Mary raced out of the bushes, snatched he and Dee's clothing off the saddles, and took off running. A bottle of sunscreen flew threw the air. It bounced off of Dee's saddle.

"Hey, you come back here," Gus shouted, breaking away from Dee and racing towards shore.

It was a waste of effort. The water was too deep and the going too slow. By the time, his bare feet hit dry ground, the women were gone.

"Now what do we do," Gus snapped.

"Well, first we finish what you started," Dee remarked dryly, "and then we put on a lot of sunscreen."

Chapter Four

Coffee, Chocolate, Cowboys… some things are just better rich.

The silver-haired moustachioed cowboy stood at the far end of the field repairing a fence, a bucket with wire, pliers, a hammer, and white electric wire fence holders sat on the ground beside him. A sweat stained Stetson shaded his eyes from the noon day sun. He finished wrapping the ends of the broken electric fence wire around each other in Maggie's stallion's paddock. Why was it the redheads always seemed to cause the most trouble?

The sound of laughter tinkled like seashell wind chimes in the air. Sam turned towards the sound and saw the ladies rein up beside the two raggedy scarecrows his grandchildren had erected last Halloween. The scarecrows overlooked the creek that ran through the center of the pasture.

Raucous laughter broke out as the ladies dismounted and began busily remodelling the scarecrows. BJ's scarecrow, the taller of the two, ended up with boobs and a red scarf draped around its neck. Jenny's scarecrow sported a faded green t-shirt with something stitched on the left breast which looked suspiciously like a Marine's regimental logo, but Sam couldn't be sure from this distance.

"Oh, boy," he muttered to himself dropping the pliers he was holding into the Rubbermaid bucket.

He lifted the bucket off the ground, and then wandered back towards the gate leading into the stallion pen. Once at the gate, he placed the bucket on the ground, crossed his arms, and waited for the ladies to finish what they were doing.

"Afternoon, Sam," Mary grinned as she rode her paint stallion past him, the two Saint Bernards stopping to lick his hand before galloping on ahead to the barn.

"Lovely day isn't it," Sylvie laughed, her eyebrows lifting, her sky-blue eyes dancing with mischief as she walked the Hanoverian past him on a loose rein. The horse's hooves were almost twice the size of Sam's hands, the earth shaking perceptibly every time they connected with the ground. Buddy swung his head towards Sam and snorted a greeting.

Sam leaned against the gate; arms still folded across his chest. Whenever Sylvie looked over her shoulder at him, his heart raced. He was hopelessly in love with her, hopeless being the key word. Their love would probably be unrequited for the remainder of their lives. It was too darned complicated to even consider.

Maggie smirked as she collected the fine boned chestnut into a tight ball as the horse pranced nervously past, sweat glistening on its neck and haunches. The whites of its eyes were more prominent than the ebony pupils. After nearly two years, Sam had just gotten the stallion to relax around him. He and the stud made eye contact as it skipped sideways, nostrils flared. Sam wanted to tell the horse to relax, the ride was over, but refrained lest Maggie go off the handle.

Zoe, ever so prim and proper, wore a white bolero jacket and a snappy Spanish style black riding hat with a wide brim, her thin aristocratic nose lifted slightly in the air, her hands steady on the double reins, as she asked the aging Andalusian to piaffe directly in front of him. The stallion danced on the spot in perfect form, one-two, one-two, haunches rippling, neck arched, head at a perfectly straight downward angle, neither over collecting into the chest nor nose pushing outwards.

They were all showing off. Whatever trouble they had gotten into, they were as happy as barn cats after a successful hunt.

Sam shook his head and pushed himself off the fence. He picked up the bucket and walked away, the ladies' laughter ringing in his ears. The joviality continued all the way to the barn.

A mare whinnied shrilly as the parade of stallions went by. He wasn't sure if it was Penny, his daughter-in-law's Quarter horse, Rosy, his granddaughter's pony, or Checkers, his cow horse, as all of them had that high pitched squeal of interest that mares all over the world trumpeted when a stud caught their interest. It wasn't Zoe's filly, Extravaganza, because she still had a foal at her side and for the most part, ignored the boys. Sam had moved the Andalusian and her foal and all the ranch horses to the back paddocks when the ladies rode out to make sure there wouldn't be any fuss, plus it was shadier and cooler behind the barn.

The old rancher sighed heavily and wandered back out towards the fields, continuing on until he came to the far pasture where two grey donkeys and one ebony mule munched away on what was left of the grass in their paddock.

One of the donkeys was missing an ear, the result of crossing paths with a couple of vicious drug smugglers. That donkey's name was Gus. The other donkey was O'Hara and the mule was named Cade after Sylvie's cheating husband. Maggie and Zoe had ridden Cade and O'Hara across the border from Mexico and couldn't bear to leave them behind. The wayward husband hadn't been seen in almost two years.

"Well, boys, how you all doing today," Sam greeted them. Gus brayed out a greeting. The other two merely looked up and then returned to grazing.

Sam laughed as he stopped to watch them eat for awhile. He was attached to the homely critters. His old reining horse, Boomer, used to be stabled with the motley crew, but he had passed last winter. Boomer, the paint stallion, and the three amigos had been inseparable. Originally, Boomer had provided companionship to Maggie's stallion, but once Boomer started to go downhill, the stallion started to fret and was constantly nipping at the old horse. It was a tough time for all.

Dust gathered on the horizon. Sam's eyes narrowed as two horsemen galloped across the ranch's pasture towards him. He briefly wondered who it was; he wasn't expecting company.

As they grew closer, he thought he recognized the horses. When they skidded to a stop in front of the kids' scarecrows, he realized who the riders were and smothered a laugh.

"Sam," Gus called, lifting a hand in greeting.

"Gus," Sam replied, scratching an imaginary itch behind one ear.

"Mr. Montana," Ranger Dee added, her voice warbling. Dee's face was as scarlet as the scarf around the lady scarecrow's spindly neck. Sam wasn't sure if it was from sunburn or embarrassment.

"Thoughtful of the ladies to leave you your underwear," Sam chortled.

"Small mercies," the ATF agent grumbled.

"Not that small," Dee joked.

Gus smirked; his jaw set in a hard line.

"They did leave us sunscreen," Dee laughed merrily.

Sam looked down at his boots as the mostly naked couple dismounted and retrieved their clothes from the straw filled scarecrows, carefully shaking off the stray strands of yellowed grass clinging to their cotton shirts and jeans before dressing.

"You can look now, Sam," Dee chuckled, taking the escapade in stride.

The rancher's shoulders shook with suppressed mirth as he looked up.

"You know, I think Emma has lunch ready if you two would like to join us," he offered.

"Maybe another time," Gus grunted, mounting the bay Quarter horse.

"I think we better just head home," Dee agreed, hopping up into the saddle.

"I think we've had enough adventure for one day," the ranger added, rubbing a gentle hand down the mustang's lathered neck.

Gus nodded good-bye to Sam before turning his horse and jogging back the way they had come, reins loose, the Quarter horse picking its own pace.

"Tell Emma I'll give her a jingle later," Dee said before loping off to catch up to her beau.

Sam rubbed the stubble on his chin and then laughed heartily. He picked up the bucket and headed back to the barn. The ladies peeked out at him from inside the barn's darkened doorway.

"Is it safe to come out," Sylvie shouted.

"That depends on who you're hiding from," he hollered.

Zoe squealed and ducked back inside the barn, Mary at her heels. Sylvie simply giggled. Maggie stood with her hands on her hips looking defiant.

Sam deposited the tool bucket inside the barn door.

Sylvie, Mary, and Zoe looked sheepishly towards him.

"You're like a pack of kids. Well, kids get just desserts. You all can look after feeding and watering your own horses after that stunt," Sam informed them, tipping his hat back on his head. He then spun on his heel and strode across the dusty yard towards the house, a smile spreading across his tanned face.

The sound of stomping feet and the screech of a rusty wheelbarrow sounded behind him. The air was so still that not even a butterfly crossed his path.

Dozer and Junior walked towards him, drool dripping from their mouths, tails wagging.

Every day at The Silver Spurs Home for Aging Cowgirls was a mystery to him, Sam mused.

***

Terri fastened her leather carry bags to the back of the sleek black 1972 1000 cc Ironhead Sporty motorcycle. She slipped a leg over the black saddle. The Sportster's chrome handlebars, muffler, and gears glistened in the sunlight. The bike was her pride and joy.

"Don't get killed on that ghastly thing," Elizabeth called from the terrace.

"I won't," Terri grinned, fastening the cheek strap on her helmet.

"Same time next year," Elizabeth said, waving goodbye.

"Wouldn't miss it for the world," Terri agreed, kicking the kickstand up and starting the Sporty's engine. The bike roared into life.

People were funny, she thought, as she revved the engine. She had thought Elizabeth had despised her when she came here. Turned out, the minister was simply having a little fun at Terri's expense. It had taken Terri a week to realize what everyone else knew instantly. A pang of regret stabbed her in the heart. She would miss the Anglican minister, but she had a funeral service to attend and a stepbrother to visit. Life was like that. There was always a balance of sorrow and joy.

Terry waved one last time to Elizabeth and gunned the bike down the gravel road leading out of the resort. She would miss this place - the quiet contemplation of life, the magnificent sunrise and sunsets over the lake, the campfire songs, the companionship of the other priests, and most of all, she would miss the healing grace of the forest. As the wind lifted the strands of the short orange hair poking out from beneath her helmet, she lowered her visor and sped off into the unknown.

The roar of the Sporty drowned out her sobs as she sped along the highway.

***

O'Hara tipped the Hilton's doorman handsomely as he left the hotel, three spiffy new suitcases waiting by the curb for the cabby to pick up.

The old man eyed the Mercedes dealership across the road from the grand hotel. From inside the dealership's display window, a cherry red AMG two-seater sports car winked at him. It was an illusion of course, but in O'Hara's opinion, it was a wink. The car was as sleek as a racehorse and prettier than any dame he had ever met.

"Hold the cab, Tomas," he told the doorman.

"Yes sir," Tomas grinned upon seeing the glint in his customer's eyes.

"Reno's not such a long drive from here, is it?" O'Hara said to the doorman.

"Two or three days, depending on how hard you push it," the doorman replied.

"I'll be back," the bowlegged gambler quipped, stepping off the curb and into the oncoming traffic, his eyes on the hot little number in the window.

Tires screeched.

Horns blared.

A huge sweeping grin spread across O'Hara's face.

The doorman waved away the cab that pulled up in front of the hotel.

Chapter Five

A stubborn horse walks behind you, an impatient horse walks in front of you, but a noble companion walks beside you.

The blood bay colt nibbled on BJ's belt buckle; the yearling's expressive gaze fascinated by the sun glinting off the silver buckle. The fifteen-year-old was as tall and gangly as the colt standing beside him. The teen favoured the Montana side of the family, not his mother's, his black hair cut short beneath the weathered white cowboy hat perched atop his head, his hazel eyes alive with intelligence.

His grandfather and mother leaned against the fence while Zoe, the colt's owner, ran a hand over the horse's sleek coat. The bright summer sun made the red-brown hair glisten like burnished copper. The colt's legs were black as a stormy night.

"If I didn't know better, I'd swear that Buddy was Expresso's father and not Desert Storm," Zoe beamed.

"He is pretty big boned, isn't he," Sam nodded, agreeing with Zoe's statement.

"And his color is magnificent," Emma added, her blue eyes as deep and colourful as the Caribbean Sea. "If he was out of Storm, I'd have thought he would have been born a chestnut."

"Not necessarily," Zoe informed them. "Zippo is Extravaganza's father, and he was born black. He didn't go grey until he was two and settled on white when he was six. That is more common than you might think."

"What about Extravaganza," Sam asked.

"Oh, she was born snow white like her mother," Zoe grinned, her brow furrowing in thought.

"You think we should have a DNA test done," BJ asked the classy older woman, bending down to pick up the colt's left rear hind hoof.

"I do," Zoe agreed. "I know it was Desert Storm we caught loose with Extravaganza when she was in heat, but I think Buddy may have surprised us. He could clear his paddock fence in a heartbeat if the desire struck him. Don't ever doubt that."

"You think he could have jumped in and out of his stallion pen without us knowing about it, grandpa," BJ asked his granddad, still sceptical.

"Possibly," Sam said, rubbing the stubble on his chin. "He's such a good-natured lumbering old fellow that it is easy to forget he's a stallion, but I've watched those videos of Sylvie competing on him and that horse can jump."

"Yes, he was a magnificent hunter in his day. That is why I wanted to meet with you privately," Zoe remarked dryly. "I am ninety percent sure this colt is Buddy's and not Desert Storm's. If he is, BJ, my decision will be much easier to make."

"I don't understand," Emma stammered, "what does that mean? What does Expresso's father have to do with anything?"

Sam glanced over at BJ. BJ understood how horse's registration worked. A breeding between a mare and a stallion had to be registered when the papers were sent in after the foal was born in order to prove bloodlines.

"It means, Emma," Zoe smiled, "that I won't have to deal with Maggie in order to decide what is best for the colt."

Wait! What? Now it was Sam's turn to wonder what Zoe was getting at.

"You aren't going to sell him, are you," BJ blurted out, his face lined with worry.

Sam reached over the fence and laid a reassuring hand on his grandson's shoulder. The colt pinned his ears back and nipped at Sam.

BJ gave a quick tug on the lead line. The colt stepped back. The colt was getting saucier and more stud-like every day. Sam had already been forced to remove the colt from his mother's side when Expresso started to play mount her. The mare was relieved, the colt not so much.

"I think I might know where Zoe is heading with this," Sam added, realization hitting him square in the face like a mosquito on a windshield.

"BJ, you are a remarkable horseman," Zoe smiled. "You are a natural. People dream of possessing the skills that you were born with. You are not just a multi-disciplined rider in reining and dressage, but you are fearless. If you set your mind to it and start learning to jump on Buddy, you could go in any direction, from dressage to hunters to eventing. How many ribbons have you already won in dressage riding Zippo? Twelve."

"Fourteen, but that was all Zippo's doing," BJ blushed.

"Not entirely," Zoe chuckled.

"I don't understand," Emma sighed. "What am I missing here?"

"I think Zoe is making you the offer of a lifetime, son," Sam advised his grandson.

"Yes, I am," Zoe chortled. "My horses love you. I am at the end of my career. It is time for Zippo to retire in earnest. Extravaganza is too flighty in the ring. She hates showing and I am not going to force her into it anymore. Now that Expresso is weaned and growing up, I plan on taking his mum out on the trails. I think she'll love it."

"It might calm her down some," Sam replied quietly.

"This young man has the makings of a superb all-around horse," Zoe said about Expresso. "He can take you anywhere you want to go plus he is already completely bonded to you, BJ. In the end, it is up to you if you want to stay a cowboy or broaden your horizons even further."

"I don't know what to say," BJ stuttered.

"Oh, my goodness," Emma cried, tears of joy forming in her eyes.

"You don't have to answer this instant," Zoe said, removing the colt's halter. "We'll get that DNA test done, quietly of course, and go from there."

"You think Maggie will want a say in it, don't you," Emma said, understanding dawning on her face.

"We all know Maggie," Zoe snorted derisively. "While we get along fine now, as Expresso develops, she could decide she wants him for herself."

"That's ludicrous," Emma gasped. "She doesn't compete anymore and she's too old to train a youngster, especially a colt as spirited as this one."

"Zoe's right, Emma, Maggie could have her own designs on the colt or expect half of whatever he's worth," Sam cautioned her, "and that is more than we can afford."

BJ stood silently in the paddock, hazel eyes down, his hand on the colt's neck.

The sound of truck tires on gravel disrupted their conversation.

"We've got a visitor. We'll discuss it more later, BJ,' Sam mumbled, turning away.

"I'm gonna stay out here with Expresso," BJ murmured wrapping an arm around the colt's neck. The colt rested its head on BJ's shoulder and closed its eyes.

Emma smiled and gave Zoe a thumb's up before running after Sam.

"Don't fret, BJ," Zoe sighed. "Whatever you decide and whatever the results of the DNA test may be, it will all work out in the end."

"Nothing to decide, ma'am," BJ whispered. "I'd love to own Expresso. I'm good with whatever discipline he decides he loves to do, even if he just wants to be a ranch horse."

"Well said, young man," Zoe whispered, her voice crackling with emotion.

***

Gus wheeled Dee's truck into the yard and parked in front of the house. As he stepped out of the cab, he saw Sam and Emma walk out of the barn and head towards them. Shortly afterwards, Zoe followed suit.

"Just the people I wanted to see," Gus grinned.

"Gus," Emma smiled, the freckles on her face seeming to dance with glee as she pushed a strand of hair out of her face.

"Hey, Em," Gus said, greeting the group warmly. "I need you guys' help."

"You need help?" Sam laughed. "Since when?"

"Nice to see you, handsome," Zoe smirked lasciviously. "Have you finally come to your senses and realized that you want someone older and more experienced in your life?"

Gus, Sam and Emma roared with laughter.

"Thanks, ma'am, but that is sort of why I'm here," Gus blushed.

"Ooooh, tell me more," Zoe teased.

"I want to ask Dee to marry me, and I have this crazy idea on how to do it," Gus said, his face reddening even more.

Emma squealed with delight.

Sam slapped Gus on the back so hard he stumbled, a wide grin on his face. "Good for you," Sam rejoiced.

"Marvellous," Zoe clapped.

"I want to send Dee on a mission into the hills only instead of finding an injured bird or a deer, she finds me instead, with a ring and flowers of course," Gus gushed. "You think that's too lame? My sister likes the idea."

"That's epic," Emma responded, drawing Gus in for a hug. "It's perfect. People think all Dee does is track down dangerous animals and give out tickets in the park, but she rescues all sorts of birds and animals."

"Not to mention one-eared donkeys," Sam added.

"What do you need us to do," Zoe asked, her eyes glinting with mischief.

"Well, my sister is on her way for a visit, and I was hoping that she'd keep Dee busy while I set it all up," Gus nodded. "I need to pick out a ring and then figure out how to get Dee riding from point A to point B and back again. I figured that I'd set up the proposal spot in the canyon where we found Tommy Cortez. That was where I fell in love with her. I don't know if you know that?"

"Oh, I think that was pretty obvious," Sam guffawed.

"What fun," Zoe giggled. "I'm in. I'll tell the girls later."

"How about we sit down with a map and figure it all out after your sister gets here," Sam offered. "She's a pastor, isn't she?"

"Yes, sir," Gus agreed.

"We could have the wedding at the ranch," Emma jumped in.

"Oh, yes, we'll decorate the yard with flowers and tents," Zoe chimed. "I can picture it now. We could do an Arabian Nights theme."

Gus' eyes bulged. His jaw clamped shut.

"Let's work on the engagement plans first, ladies," Sam laughed.

"Party pooper," Zoe sulked.

"Don't worry, Gus, we'll help you," Emma consoled the ATF agent. "We won't tell Jenny until we have to. She's not the best at keeping secrets. Zoe, make sure you talk to the ladies in private. Sam and I will talk to BJ."

"Jenny's not going to like that," Sam grumbled. "I keep telling her there are no secrets in our house, but I see your point. The whole town would know by tomorrow. Dee would have everyone whispering behind her back. That wouldn't go over well."

"Thanks," Gus beamed. "I have to go. I told Dee I was just going to gas up the truck."

"You better get then," Sam ordered.

"I'll call," Gus added. He did a quick about face and raced back to the truck.

Sam, Emma and Zoe waved to the love-struck agent as he wheeled the truck around and headed back the way he had come.

"And another one bites the dust," Sam joked.

Emma slapped him playfully on the arm.

"Maybe Gus' engagement will spur that man of yours to get busy and pop the question, Emma," Zoe purred.

"Maybe you should whisper more than sweet nothings in his ear," Sam grinned.

"Don't you dare go hinting that to him, either of you, you hear me," Emma growled.

"You have to admit, a double wedding at the ranch would be fun," Zoe said, eying Emma.

"Oh, you two," Emma snorted, storming across the yard.

"Me thinks the lady doth protest too much," Sam chuckled.

"Me thinks you're right," Zoe agreed, wrapping an arm under Sam's as they walked towards the house. "Maybe it's time you did something about it too."

"Zoeeee," Sam grumbled. "She's still married. Remember?"

"She could file for divorce en absentia, or however they do it," Zoe murmured. "I could ask my lawyer. I am sure there is something that can be done. If Cade is alive after all this time, he's left Sylvie in the dust. I wouldn't put it past him, and I only slept with him once."

Sam snorted in amusement.

Emma disappeared into the house. The screen door slammed shut behind her.

"I suppose it couldn't hurt to look into it," Sam replied thoughtfully.

"Why Sam Montana, I'm speechless. I'll call my lawyer this afternoon," Zoe said, leaning her head on Sam's shoulder. "Wouldn't it be wonderful for you and Sylvie to finally get some closure?"

Sam remained silent. There was nothing else to say.

***

O'Hara sped along the highway, heading towards the coast. The little red sports coupe zoomed along, its suspension and tires hugging the road as he opened it up.

A mountain rose high into the sky on the one side of the highway while brown grasses baked lifeless amidst the sage brush and empty spaces graced the other. He passed one ranch after the other, the pastures furrow, the last cut of hay long since having been brought in.

The blue sky above was bright and cloudless.

He turned off the radio. He'd listened to enough country and bible-thumpers in the past two days to last him a lifetime. Right now, the wind rushing past him on the highway and the purr of the sports car's engine was orchestra enough for him.

Suddenly, a dark grey SUV blasted out of nowhere around the curve behind him, barrelling up to within a foot of his rear bumper before brake lights flared and it slowed down.

Jerk! O'Hara grimaced.

The old man put his foot to the floor, wanting to put some distance between his new sportscar and the SUV. The little Mercedes shot forward. The SUV matched its pace. They continued like that for a few miles.

"Crazy patchy twat," O'Hara fumed.

O'Hara slowed and waved the SUV around him. There was no point arguing with a madman. He wasn't in that much of a hurry to get to Reno.

He let his foot off the gas, slowing to sixty, and then fifty, and finally forty miles an hour. There was lots of room to pass. No one was coming in the opposite direction. The two of them were the only vehicles on the road.

The SUV pulled out to pass. As soon as the grey Suburban paralleled the sports car, it swerved towards the driver's side door. The old man hit the breaks and slid to a stop, fishtailing off the road and onto the shoulder.

"HEY," the old man screamed. "You idiot!"

The SUV pulled onto the gravel shoulder in front of him, the driver waving a hand in apology out the window. The SUV's taillights glowed red.

"Stupid sod," O'Hara mumbled.

Frustrated, O'Hara waved back as if nothing had happened. No point in getting a gun waved in his face.

He started to pull back onto the highway when the driver stepped out of the Suburban, leaving his door open, effectively blocking O'Hara's safe passage from the shoulder on to the narrow highway. The man wore a colourful Western shirt with a Navaho motif on the front. A handgun was in one hand. He bounced the gun casually off his thigh as he stalked towards the sports car.

Shock stilled the retired steeplechase jockey's heart as he recognized the cold grey eyes of the man walking towards him. Silently, O'Hara cursed himself for the foibles that led to his ultimate demise.

Chapter Six

Our greatest glory is not in never falling, but in rising every time we fall.
Confucious

A sharp pain tore through Terri's back as she pulled over onto the shoulder of the highway, the Harley's rumble going from a lion-like roar to a humble purr as the sporty slowed down.

She loved her bike, but her lower back and kidneys took a pounding along lesser maintained highways like the one she was on now. Sleeping on a leaky air mattress on a barn floor hadn't helped much either.

Terri had awakened to a hairy face examining hers, gobs of wet grain dripping from its mouth onto her chin, and warm fetid breath tickling her nostrils. It turned out that she hadn't been called in to do a eulogy for her old biker buddy but to counsel his grieving horse. The horse hadn't eaten in days. Said horse had enjoyed her company all night. The bikers were thrilled to see it eating again. Terri had a few objections, but nothing that a hot shower hadn't fixed.

The Lord worked in mysterious ways indeed, Terri grinned, as she shut the Harley down and coasted off the highway.

She parked the bike and strolled into the bushes. She looked around to make sure nobody could see her from the road and tugged down her jeans. Relief flooded through her as her bladder emptied. Her back pain eased right away, and she had a magnificent view.

The peak that rose majestically above the highway was ragged and intimidating. Tall Douglas fir and scattered pine trees marched from the base of the rocky mountain to the highway. The sky above was bright blue; not even a wisp of a cloud marred the scenic view.

It was good to be on her home turf and not in a camp surrounded by barbed wire and guard outposts. Freedom, oh how we take it for granted, she thought.

A funny hiccupping squawk startled her out of her reverie. She yanked up her jeans and then followed the angry series of squawks, pushing aside bushes and brambles until she came upon a small clearing. The smell hit her first. It was a familiar scent, one of death and dying, bitter and rank like ammonia and fresh dung. She didn't expect to find it here in this beautiful wilderness. Trepidation quickened her step.

Terri crossed herself, sending up a prayer that it be a dead animal and not something much worse.

Her heart broke when she saw the cherry red Mercedes convertible parked in the middle of the clearing, a body lying on the ground beside it. A seething mass of turkey buzzards fought over the corpse.

"Hey, get out of here," she screamed at the large birds. A dozen set of golden eyes turned towards her.

Terri raced forward, flapping her arms to get the birds moving. The birds flew angrily away, only to land a dozen paces from the body. If looks could kill, Terri would be lying on the ground beside the lifeless elderly gentleman. Terri had seen enough death and destruction overseas to not be alarmed by the poor soul with the bullet hole in his forehead, but the sight brought tears to her eyes. At least the birds hadn't been there long.

The army pastor mumbled a prayer before striding forward. She reached the car and popped open the small trunk, hoping to find a blanket or a tarp to cover the body with. The smell of horse manure greeted her.

How odd, she thought, *horse manure of all things!*

She hauled the old man's suitcases out of the trunk and placed them on the ground, not worrying about leaving fingerprints as she still wore her leather riding gloves. She immediately discovered where the smell was coming from. A worn brown floor length oilskin Aussie slicker lay beneath the suitcases. The coat was old, the canvas cracked in places, but the top shoulders had been recently oiled. Tucked alongside the coat was a pair of manure crusted rubber muck boots.

Terri sighed wearily as she pulled the coat out of the trunk and gingerly covered the dead man with it. The turkey buzzards ruffled their feathers and watched her every move.

"Buzz off," she ordered the birds. "You're done here."

The turkey buzzards ignored her.

Terri yanked off her gloves and pulled her cell phone from her pocket. She thumbed through the phone's address book and tapped on her brother's name.

"Hey, where are you," Gus' rich alto voice boomed over the phone.

"Well, I'm on the highway below the mountain a short distance from the turnoff to Dee's place according to my GPS," Terri replied.

"You break down?" Gus asked worriedly. "I can come with Dee's pickup."

"That's not the problem," she said. "I stopped for a pee and found a body."

"You what?"

"Yep, that's me, preacher, counsellor, skinny dipper, horse whisperer, and dead guy detector," she groaned.

"I'm on my way," Gus said. "Don't touch anything."

"It's a little too late for that," Terri advised him. "The buzzards got to him first. I put his coat over him so they wouldn't do any more damage."

"I'm on my way," Gus groaned. "I'll be there in about ten minutes."

"I'll meet you on the highway after I run off the ambulance chasers again," she drawled.

Terri ended the call and stepped back. She eyed the birds. The buzzards eyed her back, their red crowns bobbing from side to side. She grinned maliciously.

With a rebel yell, Terri raced towards them, eyes blazing, arms swinging, righteous fury at full throttle. The buzzards flew off, wings beating furiously as they scrambled into the air away from the crazy woman.

***

Three of the sheriff's deputies cordoned off the crime scene with yellow and black police tape while Sheriff Cole Trane and Gus listened to Terri perform a rudimentary grace over the body, hats in hand. Terri stood inside her previous tracks, two paces away from the covered corpse.

"May God bless you and keep you, may God's face shine upon you and be gracious unto you, may God look upon you with kindness and give you peace, amen," Terri concluded, snapping the bible shut.

"Amen," Cole, Gus and the three deputies said in unison.

"Thanks, pastor," Cole nodded.

"That was lovely, sis," Gus agreed.

Terri cautiously backed up, trying to continue to step in her previous tracks to preserve the crime scene, although the turkey buzzards really had made a mess of it.

"It will be another couple of hours before the CSI team gets here. I'm leaving the body covered until then. You two don't have to wait around since I've already got your statement, Terri," Cole stated.

"Sounds good, Cole, but keep me in the loop, will you?" Gus asked the sheriff. "I don't like the thought of Dee riding alone in the Park if there is a psycho running around loose. She got called out a couple of hours ago to check into an injured deer that was reported up by the old mine."

"Hey, what about me," Terri chimed.

"I don't want you riding around alone right now either," Gus reaffirmed.

"We don't see many killings like this around here, pastor," the sheriff said, pushing his Stetson back on his head. "I'm sorry this is your first impression of our piece of paradise."

"Wasn't your fault, sheriff," Terri nodded.

"That's good of you," the sheriff conceded. "I'd appreciate any help I can get on this, Gus. This whole scene isn't right. Why would the killer leave the car and body so close to the highway like this unless the killer was solo and couldn't drive the car away? And why not bury the body to hide it?"

"Killer may have thought this place was so remote the body wouldn't be found this fast," Gus noted. "It means he isn't local. Even though it looks like a professional hit, the killer may be a rank amateur."

"Or the killer wanted to make a statement," Terri added. "We saw enough of that overseas, didn't we, bro?"

"We did," Gus sighed, a grim look passing over his face.

"Anyway, like I said, you guys skedaddle. I'll give you a call after the forensic team has been and gone," Cole continued. "Samantha is tracking down the car owner's name for me. We'll go from there."

Cole's cell phone rang.

"Speak of the devil," Cole mumbled. "What'd you find, Sam?"

Terri looked questioningly at her brother. Gus shrugged. It wasn't his case. He was ATF, not sheriff's department. He'd help where he could.

Cole turned his back on them and spoke softly into the phone. His gaze darted back to the cadaver in the dirt, his cheeks reddening as he continued to speak to the dispatcher.

"That doesn't look good," Terri whispered to Gus.

"No, it doesn't," he nodded. "I wonder what's going on."

Cole turned back towards them. "I don't want anyone in here but forensics," Cole shouted to his deputies after he hung up. "And I mean no one!"

"Yes, sir," came the chorus of replies.

"You guys need to leave now," Cole ordered them, his voice hardening.

"What's going on, Cole," Gus glared, not liking the sheriff's tone.

"I can't say, Gus," the sheriff replied sternly. "I need you and your sister out of here, right now. You'll hear when everyone else does."

Gus bristled, his jaw tightening, eyes narrowing as he bit back a nasty retort. Terri knew her brother better than anyone. He didn't like being told what to do. She placed a reassuring hand on one arm. His brown eyes met hers. A nod of understanding passed between them. Whatever the sheriff had just found out made him go from howdy-doody-can-you-help-me to don't-mess-with-me-or-I'll-put-you-behind-bars in an instant.

"I'll be at Dee's for a few days if you need anything more," Terri calmly informed the sheriff.

"You can reach either of us there at any time," Gus reaffirmed.

"Thanks," Cole's voice softened.

Gus and Terri headed back up the trail that Terri had used on the way in. Her brother held up the police tape for Terri to duck underneath.

"Sorry, Gus," Cole waved to them. "It's too close to home for me to talk about. You understand, right?"

Gus shrugged and waved the sheriff off before slipping under the tape and departing the scene alongside his sister.

***

The hamburger Cole had eaten for lunch threatened to repeat itself as he lifted the coat off the body and examined the bullet hole in the centre of its forehead. In the ten years he had spent as sheriff, he had only dealt with one other murder case and that was a domestic situation, most deaths he attended being caused by bad drivers, icy road conditions, or inexperienced hunters.

Cole stepped forward and lifted the oilskin coat so he could see the face of the dead man. He grimaced. It was Cade O'Hara.

Maybe he needed the uncheck the 'he hadn't seen this before' box. It was a conundrum for sure. Sylvie O'Hara had confessed to killing her husband in a jealous rage two years ago, but then so had Cade's mistress, Maggie Carroll. The ladies had both thought they were the ones who had strangled him to death. Maggie and her accomplice, Zoe Puddicombe, had tossed him out a second story window and used a wheelbarrow to roll him into the barn. Sylvie then moved the body, leaving it in the outhouse at the back of the Montana's farm. If it was true, and Cole had no reason to doubt their recounts of the night in question, the body in front of him shouldn't be Cade O'Hara. So, how did a dead man mysteriously get up and walk away without anyone seeing him? And, more importantly, where had he spent the last two years?

Cole gently placed the coat back over the body. He straightened up and rubbed his chin, considering his options: tell the ladies outright that he had found Cade's body and study their reactions, take each one separately to the morgue to view the body and see what kind of fireworks ensued, or keep it to himself until he got a court order to examine Cade's bank accounts to see what kind of activity had taken place. The other question nagging at him was where Cade got the money to purchase the cute little Mercedes. The care cost more than three times Cole's annual salary.

He didn't like his options. Trouble was brewing. The residents at *The Silver Spurs Home for Aging Cowgirls* were tough old broads capable of handling gun wielding bandits, bumbling kidnappers, dangerous felons, and fifteen-hundred-pound stallions without breaking a sweat. No sane man would cross any one of them.

Cole chewed his bottom lip, hoping that the reappearance of Sylvie's cheating husband wouldn't destroy his relationship with Emma Montana. He had been working up the courage to propose.

"Tarnation," he muttered. "She's going to hate me."

***

"What was that all about," Terri whispered fiercely when they were out of range of the sheriff and his deputies.

"I don't know, but I'm going to find out," her brother whispered back.

"What did you do," she asked, her face reddening. Leave it to her brother to not let well enough alone.

"I may have inadvertently snapped a picture of the car's license plate," Gus grinned, attaching the picture of the plate number in a message to his partner at the office.

"Naughty boy," Terri giggled.

"You want me to follow you, or you want to put the Harley in the back of the truck," Gus asked as they pushed through the last of the brush and made their way out onto the highway.

"I'll follow you," Terri grinned. "I don't think there is a killer out there gunning for a preacher on a Harley."

"You never know," Gus snorted.

"Naw, that didn't look like a random killing to me," Terri squeaked.

"You've been watching too much TV," Gus chortled.

"Experience, bro, and you know it. That was a hit if I ever saw one."

"Yeah, it was," her brother nodded. "The old man pissed in someone's cornflakes."

Three police vehicles, the sheriff's Suburban, Dee's three-quarter ton battered green GMC pick up truck, and Terri's Harley lined the highway. Word had spread like wildfire that there was something going on out on Highway 4. The deputy left to stand guard waved the convoy of lookie-loos through.

Gus' phone dinged as a message came in.

Gus read the message.

"Oh, man," Gus exclaimed. "That explains everything."

"What does," Terri asked, eagerly.

"The owner of that little Mercedes is Cade O'Hara," Gus mumbled, looking up from his phone. "He's supposed to be dead."

"Well, he is now," Terri agreed simply.

Chapter Seven

Just because you can jump a fence going north doesn't mean you can jump in going south.

"So, what are you going to do," Dee asked Gus later in the day.

"It's not my case," Gus replied, leaning against the kitchen counter. "I'd be stepping on the sheriff's toes big time if I called Emma and told her the body found on Highway Four was Cade O'Hara, plus I never met the man, so even if I had examined the body, I couldn't say if it was him or not."

"Gus is right. The car may be registered to Mr. O'Hara, but the body might be someone completely different," Terri agreed.

Dee stood with her back to the sink, still dressed in her khaki-coloured ranger uniform, her long black hair tied behind her head in a ponytail. A frown creased her tanned face.

"I'm going to pour myself a drink," Gus declared, pushing away from the counter.

"Me too," Dee sighed, rubbing her eyes. "Do you drink, Terri? I can put on the kettle and make a pot of tea."

Gus and Terri grinned.

"Well in John's gospel Jesus' first miracle was turning water into wine, so...," Terri paused. "A glass of wine would be great, unless you have tequila?"

"We've got tequila," Gus replied, his eyes twinkling.

"I love your sister already," Dee blurted out.

Gus and Terri burst out laughing as Gus retrieved a bottle of Don Julio from a kitchen cabinet.

"Wait until she has a couple of tequilas in her, you might change your mind," Gus joked.

"Hey," Terri objected in mock anger.

Terri grinned. She wasn't a big drinker; rarely drank in fact, but when she did, tequila was her poison of choice. She looked over at her brother, bumping heads with Dee while reaching into the liquor cabinet. They both stood up, laughing, red spots on their foreheads where they banged into each other. Gus was the one good thing that came out of growing up in the foster system. They were like Peter' Pan's Lost Boys when they pinkie swore to be brother and sister forever.

Dee grabbed three shot glasses from the top of the cabinet and placed then on the table while Gus retrieved the tequila. The ranger sat down at the table beside Terri. Gus poured out three fingers of tequila; one into each shot glass, and then took a seat beside his girlfriend-slash-soon-to-be-fiancé.

Terri had never seen her brother so happy. It lightened her heart. Dee was good for him, and she could see why. She had the feeling that she and Dee were going to be the best of friends.

"I don't envy Cole," Gus sighed, lifting his glass. "He's got a tough job ahead of him."

"Yeah, if the dead guy is Cade, I'd hate to be the one to have to tell Sylvie," Dee agreed, lifting her own glass, "and Maggie too."

"I forgot about that," Gus hissed.

Terri felt the tension rise around the table. She knew Sylvie was Cade's wife, but who was Maggie?

"You know, this reminds me of my favourite quote from the bible," Terri said, switching instinctively to counsellor mode. "Micah 6:8, 'What does God want from us? To seek justice, live kindly, and walk humbly with God'. Whoever that man is I stumbled upon, let us pray that he has found his peace and his killer caught quickly and justice be served."

"Amen to that, sis," Gus agreed, clinking his glass against Terri's.

"Amen," Dee echoed, joining the toast.

***

Cole knocked briefly on the Montana's front door, and then walked into the house. He wasn't expected, but Emma always got mad at him when he waited at the door after knocking, insisting that he was family and family didn't wait to be invited in.

Huh, he paused: *maybe later he should give that idea some thought. Was that a hint? He had been thinking of proposing to her for a couple of weeks now but kept waiting for the right time. Of course, the right time never seemed to happen.*

Emma was in the kitchen cooking as always. The room was warm and smelled of cinnamon and apple pie. Pastry shells lined the counter. Two cooked pies sat cooling on baking racks on the side counter.

"Cole," she beamed, her cheeks flushed, "what a pleasant surprise."

Cole removed his hat and kissed her on the cheek, his heart rate rising. Emma's mop of copper colored hair was tied behind her head. He desperately wanted to let it down and run his fingers through it. Cole fought the urge to sweep her into his arms and inhale the womanly scent of her, but this wasn't a social visit. The thought brought his ardour to a stand still.

"Sam around?" he asked sombrely.

"He's working in his bedroom," Emma said, looking questioningly at Cole. "You know him. He is religious about keeping track of the cattle. A couple of late calves were born this week."

"That's good. I'm glad the herd is doing well. Is Sylvie here? I didn't see her truck outside."

"Maggie and Zoe took it into town to get their hair done and pick up a couple of bags of horse pellets for Sam in the process," Emma offered. "Why?"

"What's with all the questions," Sam drawled, entering the kitchen.

Cole did an about face. He hadn't heard Sam's approach. Sweat broke out on his brow. He gulped down the unrest that settled like battery acid in his stomach. All thoughts of romance were swept away in the tidal wave of scrutiny directed his way by Sam Montana.

Cole looked into the lined face of the old man in front of him, brown eyes hooded with concern, casually twirling one end of his long moustache. Sam was one of those men whose character and presence commanded attention, a born leader. If Cole ever needed advice, Sam Montana was the man he would turn to.

Cole swallowed.

Sam loved Sylvie O'Hara. It was the town's worst kept secret.

"I heard you come in," Sam acknowledged. "It ain't Saturday or Sunday so it must be important. Of course, you getting all googly-eyed over my daughter-in-law is par for the course."

The smile on Sam's face disappeared when Cole didn't respond.

"I'm sorry, Sam, this is official business," Cole stammered. "I need to speak to Sylvie… preferably alone."

Cole straightened his shoulders and tried to steady his nerves.

"What on earth for?" Emma queried, wiping her hands on a dish towel.

The look the old cowboy gave Cole would freeze a lake in August. It was all Cole could do to meet his withering gaze.

"I'll get her," Sam's baritone voice rumbled. "She's in her room."

Sam disappeared into the living room. His footsteps were as silent as a mountain lion's. Cole heard a soft murmur of voices and then silence.

"Cole, why you need to speak to Sylvie alone," Emma pleaded. "Is it serious? Did something happen to Maggie and Zoe? Is that it?"

"I'm sorry, Em," Cole mumbled. "Honestly, I can't say anything yet."

Sam returned to the kitchen.

"You can talk to Sylvie in her bedroom, but she insists I be there," Sam stated, his tone brooking no argument.

Emma gasped, a sudden realization coming over her. Her hand flew to her mouth. The timer went off. She quickly turned to remove the last apple pie from the oven.

Cole took that moment to escape her scrutiny. Emma was no fool; she had figured it out.

Cole walked alongside Sam through the house to Sylvie's bedroom which was conveniently located on the ground floor beside Sam's.

"Mrs O'Hara," Cole stuttered, twirling his Stetson in his hands as he approached Sylvie's bedroom door.

Sam brushed by him and went to stand beside Sylvie. Sylvie's piercing gaze met his as she sat in a blue winged back chair facing the door. The colour of the chair matched her eyes. She sighed wearily and put down the book she was reading.

"There's only one reason you'd want to talk to me alone. You found him, didn't you?"

"We did," Cole answered cautiously. Over the last two years, he had discovered that the ladies at the Montana ranch were not to be trifled with.

"I need you to identify the body. DNA evidence would help as well. I know it's been a long time. By any chance, do you have Cade's toothbrush still or maybe a hair comb?"

"If you need DNA evidence, why do you need Sylvie to identify the body?" Sam asked briskly. "Seems contrary, is all."

"It ain't some mummy I'm gonna have to look at, is it?" Sylvie's voice warbled.

"No ma'am, it's not a mummy," Cole answered cracking a smile. "A body was found on the county road. The vehicle found with it is registered to your husband. I have a procedure to follow, that's all."

"So, he really did survive," Sam harrumphed.

"You know what my husband looks like," Sylvie snapped. "Why do I have to identify him?"

"Procedure, ma'am," Cole replied simply.

"Let's get this over with then," Sylvie grunted, pushing herself out of the chair.

Cole blushed, twirling his hat even harder. Sam eyed him even more coldly.

"As for the stuff you wanted, well, that's not so easy. I read a book that said if you wanted to get over someone or some trauma in your life, perform a cleansing ceremony," the not so frail woman grinned maliciously. "I took that bit of advice to heart."

"Damnable woman, you darned near set the house on fire," Sam guffawed. "I told her the next time she wanted to clear her mind to do it in the riding ring out behind the barn."

"Well, I didn't think I had that much baggage," Sylvie shrugged.

Sam rolled his eyes, his face softening as he looked at the spitfire of a woman standing beside him.

Yep, it was clear Sam loved Sylvie O'Hara, Cole thought. There was no doubt in Cole's mind. With a start, he realized that he was going to have to add his girlfriend's father-in-law to his suspect list.

Cole shook his head in consternation. Cade O'Hara just had to die on his section of highway!

***

"Yep, that's my husband," Sylvie sighed, leaning heavily against Sam.

Cole stood beside the young male morgue attendant. The attendant slipped the sterile sheet back over the body.

"Thank you, Mrs O'Hara," the attendant said. "Once the sheriff gives us the okay, you can let the coroner know where you would like us to deliver your husband's remains to."

"Is straight to Hell an option?" Sylvie smirked.

The attendant gaped at the widow O'Hara.

Cole wasn't surprised. From what Emma told him, Cade had treated his wife miserably. Sam stood off to one side, his eyes downcast. That alone spoke volumes. It also went to motive.

***

A host of emotions churned inside Sylvie's breast ranging from rage to sadness, bitterness to relief. The sight of Cade, her husband of forty years, a man she had once thought of as Samson to her Delilah, lying grey and slack upon a cold steel shelf, a neat circular hole in his forehead, dragged up feelings she wasn't prepared for.

"You going to be okay?" Sam murmured.

"I'm not sure," she replied, ashen faced. Part of her wanted to throw herself over her husband's body and weep rivers of tears, for her, for him, for their lost daughter, and for the life they could have had but hadn't. Another part of her wanted to choke him to death one more time.

She watched thin lipped as the attendant slid the body back inside the cooler. The sound of the rollers scraping on the underside of the steel tray grated on her nerves.

"I'm sorry," she whispered to Cade as he disappeared into the cold darkness.

Sam offered her a Kleenex. She took it gratefully and dabbed at her eyes.

"Just to be clear, you are confirming that the body you just viewed is your husband, Cade Rupert O'Hara," Cole reiterated.

"Yes, that's Cade," Sylvie croaked.

She took a deep breath and let it out slowly, shaken to the core.

"I'd like to go home now, Cole," Sylvie said, pushing Sam's hand away as he tried to hold hers.

Sylvie didn't want anyone's pity, especially Sam's.

"Yes, ma'am, you're free to go," Cole nodded.

The handsome young sheriff then escorted Sylvie and Sam out of the morgue and back to their vehicle. The yellow glow cast from the parking lot lights made everyone's skin look sallow. Night had fallen. A chill was in the air. Sylvie shivered.

"Cade's winter coat might still be in the front compartment of the horse trailer," Sylvie informed Cole before climbing into the passenger seat of Sam's pick-up truck. "I'll check when we get home."

"That would be a big help," Cole responded. "I'm sorry about all this, Sylvie."

"I know, Cole," Sylvie smiled weakly. "You're just doing your job."

Cole nodded and put his cowboy hat back on. He and Sam shook hands. Sylvie was glad to see there were no hard feelings. She didn't want any of this to affect Emma, Sam, or the children. She loved Emma like a daughter and was happy to be one of Jenny's cowgirl grandmas.

"I told Emma not to tell the ladies," the sheriff drawled. "I should follow you back to the ranch and tell them myself, but ..."

"If you think Maggie or Zoe shot Cade, you're barking up the wrong tree," Sam growled, jumping to a conclusion.

Sylvie started. It hadn't even occurred to her that she and Maggie were suspects. The idea was ludicrous. Sylvie had already confessed to killing Cade once. Leave it to Sam to be one step ahead of her.

"And don't you dare say it's procedure," Sam finished.

Cole shook his head in consternation.

"No sir, I'm pretty sure none of the ladies had anything to do with this, but I still need to talk to Miss Carroll and Mrs Puddicombe," Cole said, "but it can wait until morning."

Sylvie blanched. The sheriff couldn't lie worth a darn. They were all suspects, even Sam.

"I got some leads to follow up on. I promise you; I'll find out who did this," the sheriff said.

Sam nodded and closed Sylvie's door gently.

Sylvie leaned back in the seat and watched Sam stride around the front of the truck to the driver's side door. Sheriff Cole Trane cut a forlorn figure as he walked across the mostly empty parking lot to the white Suburban with the sheriff's decal on the side door. She wondered how Maggie was going to react to the news that Cade's body had been found. Maggie loved Cade as much as Sylvie had. She was going to tell her anyway. She had as much a right to know as Sylvie did. It was not going to be a pleasant night.

Chapter Eight

Life is like a wild horse. You ride it or it rides you.

"Grandpa, you look sad," ten-year-old Jenny Montana exclaimed as Sam and Sylvie shuffled into the kitchen where Jenny sat at the table with her mother, brother, and Mary playing a round of Go Fish.

"He's not anymore seeing that you're winning," Sylvie joked half-heartedly.

Jenny grinned happily and ran a hand gleefully through the pile of poker chips sitting on the table in front of her.

"There's a fresh pot of coffee over there," Emma nodded towards the side table where several upturned mugs sat beside a bowl of sugar and a large coffee thermos. "You look like you could use a cup."

"You guys do look like something the cat dragged in," Mary added, looking up from her handful of cards.

"I feel like it," Sylvie snorted.

Sam looked at the clock. It was nine o'clock.

"How about after Sylvie and me fix us a coffee, the family go out to the barn and give the horses an extra feed. I want to double check all the saddles and roping gear too.

I think we'll go fetch the cattle down from the north pasture tomorrow. What do you think, princess?"

"You mean I can go to," Jenny shouted, jumping up from the table, her cards and poker chips scattering.

"I reckon you can," Sam grinned, "so long as you think Rosie is up to it."

"It's a little early, isn't it" BJ asked his grandfather, puzzled.

"Farmer's Almanac says weather's going to turn," Sam nodded. "Never argue with the Almanac."

"I've got an idea," Mary offered, "why don't you ride Patch, Jenny. Those Black Angus of your grandpas are bigger than Rosie. Patch loves to cut cows. You think you can handle him?"

"Really? You mean it?" Jenny gushed.

"I wouldn't offer if I didn't," Mary smirked.

"Can I, grandpa? Can I ride Patch on a cattle drive?" Jenny looked expectantly at her grandfather.

"Normally, there would be no way I'd let a girl your age ride a stallion, but given that it is Patch, if your feet can reach the stirrups, you can ride him."

"Woohoo," Jenny cried, punching BJ on the arm before racing around the table to hug Mary.

"Go on out to the barn with your sister," Emma told her son. "We'll be there shortly."

"Last one there is a rotten egg," BJ teased his sister.

Jenny screamed out the door, BJ jogging slowly after her. The teen always let his sister win.

"So, give," Mary said, clearing the cards off the table.

Sylvie wrapped an arm around her friend, hugging her tight. Tears trickled unbidden from Sylvie's eyes.

"Whoa, shhhh, shhhh, what's going on?" Mary asked, wrapping her arms around her friend.

Emma glanced worriedly at Sam. He smiled sadly as he walked by her on the way to the coffee urn. He poured out two cups of coffee, leaving one black and adding double sugar and cream to the other. Sam placed the cream and sugar mug on the table in front of Sylvie.

"In case you need more," he smiled sadly.

"I'll ask the ladies to come down and then meet you in the barn, Sam," Emma offered.

Sam nodded. Coffee cup in hand, he spun on his heel and headed for the door, his face and body taught with tension.

The last time Emma had seen her father-in-law so done in was after Gus had arrived bearing the American flag that had covered Cleve's coffin.

Emma had just placed a foot on the stair to go upstairs when she heard a heart wrenching sob coming from the kitchen. Tears welled in her eyes. Emma brushed them away; she knew exactly how Sylvie was feeling.

***

Jenny skipped down the aisle, tossing a flake of hay over the horses' stall doors, all except for the colt named Expresso. BJ took care of the youngster himself.

The horses backed away when they saw Jenny coming. They had learned from experience the little girl's aim was sometimes off. The only horse that didn't was Sylvie's stallion, Buddy. The worst Jenny could do to him was hit him in the chest with a flake of alfalfa.

Sam let the kids handle the feed and watering while he walked through the barn to the tack room. He slumped into a chair and sipped his coffee, waiting for Emma to arrive.

BJ's head appeared in the doorway.

"Grandpa, are you alright?"

"Just tired, grandson," Sam said, forcing a smile. He wasn't about to discuss his mixed emotions over Sylvie's new widowhood status with his teenaged grandson. He was struggling with it himself. On the one hand, he could now openly express his love for Cade's wife; on the other hand, he never wished harm to the man. Sam still had a hard time believing that Cade had lived through the ordeal the women had put him through; plus, Sam had seen Cade's body with his own eyes. Dead was dead. How on earth did a dead man get up and walk out of an outhouse?

"I'll tell you what's happened when your mother gets here."

"I'm here," Emma announced.

Sam stood up and joined BJ, Jenny and Emma in the aisle.

Emma wrapped an arm around Jenny's shoulder. Jenny grinned up at her, her peach-coloured hair dotted with alfalfa sprouts. Sam couldn't help but grin. Mother and daughter looked so much alike. An orchestra of freckles played across their cheeks.

"I'm afraid I have some sad news," Sam rumbled, raising a hand for Jenny to hold her questions until he was finished. His granddaughter veritably vibrated beneath her mother's arm, but then right from a baby, Jenny was never still. "Mr. O'Hara has been found."

"He has? Is he coming for dinner?" Jenny screeched her voice as sharp as nails on a blackboard. "I got a bone to pick with him. He never said goodbye when he left."

"Jenny, stop," Emma scolded her daughter. "Let your grandfather finish."

BJ leaned against Expresso's stall. The colt nibbled his hair. The teen brushed the horse's lips away, his head down, crestfallen, sensing there was worse news to come.

"Mr O'Hara has passed on," Sam replied.

"Nooooo," Jenny wailed. "You're lying! Cade can't be gone! He's my friend."

"Jenny, stop," Emma crooned, holding her daughter tightly. "Grandpa wouldn't lie to you."

"What happened," BJ asked quietly, his eyes meeting his grandfather's.

Cade may have been a womanizer and an alcoholic, but he was a likable fellow, full of life, and good with the kids. Sam didn't approve of his morals, but he couldn't fault Cade for Cade's love of Sam's grandchildren. BJ's eyes reflected that. Sam wouldn't destroy the good image the kids had of the man.

"I don't want to get into the details," Sam replied hoarsely. "What I want us to do is remember him. Do you remember taking Mr O'Hara shopping for a cowboy hat and cowboy boots so he could be a real cowboy, Jenny?"

"Yeah," Jenny sniffled. "He was lit! He did this like catwalk thing wearing a lady's pink cowboy hat and sparkly purple shirt. Everyone was in stitches, even Mr Wiley and he doesn't smile ever."

"Cade was entertaining, I'll give him that," Emma laughed, wiping the tears from her eyes.

"And he loved your song about Mike," Sam offered.

"He wouldn't stop singing it. It drove me nuts," BJ smiled. "Every time I tried showing him how to rope, he'd start singing that darned song and I'd miss the fence post. He kept threatening to record it and get the judge to play it at the next dressage competition."

The Montana family laughed and laughed as they spoke of the funny things Cade had done during his short stay at the ranch.

Sam made a rash decision. He hoped he wouldn't live to regret it, but it seemed like the perfect time. Luckily, school was two weeks away. She could keep a secret that long, right?

"On a happier note, someone has asked for our help," Sam said, looking pointedly at Emma. Emma raised her eyebrows questioningly. Sam pushed on. "Now we don't usually keep secrets, but with this one we have to."

"You sure about this," Emma mouthed to him over top of Jenny's head.

Sam nodded.

"Gus is going to propose to Dee," Sam said. "And he needs our help."

"Really," Jenny blurted out, breaking away from her mother, and dashing into his arms.

Out of sight, out of mind, Sam guessed. The last two years may have passed in a blink of an eye to Sam and Sylvie, but Cade's disappearance probably felt like an eternity to Jenny. Already, she seemed to have moved on, but kids were a lot more resilient than adults.

"I've had some time to think on that," BJ offered. "I thought we could start with Ranger Dee getting the coordinates to find a wounded animal like Gus suggested, but when she gets there, she finds one of us with new coordinates to follow instead. We get her to ride all over the mountain from place to place receiving new coordinates from different people. She'll know something is up, but not exactly what. Geocaching is what made me think of it. There's a club at school."

"That's brilliant," Emma agreed. "We could get the ladies involved too."

"Oh, me, me, I get to be at the end," Jenny giggled, jumping up and down.

"No, Gus will be at the end, honey," Emma grinned. "He's the one with the ring."

"Oh, right, then can I be at the start," Jenny beamed.

"I'm sure we can arrange that," Sam chortled. "In the meantime, I'll text Gus your idea, BJ. Now, let's get those saddles cleaned and ropes checked."

"Ahhhh," Jenny whined.

"You want to join the cattle drive or not," Sam rumbled.

"Yessss," his granddaughter whimpered, before breaking into an impish grin. "Maybe I can take something of Cade's on the cattle drive with us? It would feel like he was there."

"That's a lovely thought, honey," Emma replied, tearing up.

Sam shook his head, his moustache twitching. He never did understand how women could flip flop from happy to sad in a split second.

Chapter Nine

The hardest thing about learning to ride is the ground!

Mary poured a shot of Bailey's Irish Cream into Sylvie's coffee cup. "Fortitude," Mary smirked.

Sylvie nodded.

"Oooh, are we going to play cards," Zoe asked, fastening her pink silk robe around her waist. "We haven't played poker in ages."

"Not tonight," Sylvie sighed.

"Then what are we doing here?" Maggie grumbled. "I'm into a particularly juicy section in my new Sarah MacLean novel."

"The Hell's Belles novel?" Zoe grinned. "Can I read it when you're done?"

"I suppose," Maggie purred, her dark eyes glittering in the glow cast by the stove's night light.

Emma had dimmed the kitchen lights when she left. It made the kitchen feel less sterile. Sylvie had appreciated the small gesture.

The moment, while awkward, was peaceful. Sylvie felt bad about shattering it.

"Hush, both of you," Mary scolded her friends. "Sylvie has some important news to share. Now, sit down!"

"Wonderful," Zoe exploded, taking her usual seat at the table. "You and Sam finally did it!"

"Noooo," Sylvie barked, shaking her head in exasperation.

"Too bad. I guess that explains why you look so down," Maggie nodded wisely, gliding into the chair beside Zoe. "It's that damn cowboy code thing, isn't it?"

"NO. This has nothing to do with Sam. Cade's dead!" Sylvie exploded, cutting Zoe and Maggie off.

"Well, of course he is darling," Maggie replied flippantly. "We just don't know where his body went."

"We do now," Sylvie groaned, rubbing the spot on her temples where a headache was forming. "He's lying on a slab in the morgue with a bullet hole in his head!"

Zoe and Maggie glanced at each other, and then at Sylvie. It was clear they thought she had lost her mind. Perhaps she had?

"Cole asked me to identify his body," Sylvie sniffed. "Sam went with me."

"I thought you were on a date," Zoe mumbled.

"Me too," Maggie agreed.

The women sat in silence for a few minutes while Zoe and Maggie digested the information. Mary had already had some time to do so.

"Oh, my," Zoe whispered, a hand going to the ruff of feathers around the collar of her nightgown. She stroked the lacy feathers casually.

"Well, I didn't kill him," Mary shrugged, breaking the silence. "I had no reason to, I wasn't sleeping with him."

"I only slept with him once," Zoe whined, squirming in her seat. "Frankly, it wasn't that exciting."

Maggie glared at the spiky-haired senior sitting beside her. Zoe moved her chair a few inches away from Maggie's intimidating stare. She'd have moved farther, but a side table stood in her way.

"I strangled him; I didn't shoot him. In all fairness, I didn't know Sylvie had already done so too," Maggie added smugly.

"I did, and I've regretted it ever since," Sylvie groaned, "although shoving your panties down his throat, Mags, was pretty satisfying."

"Huh," the ladies said in unison.

"So, the question is," Mary began.

"Who killed Cade?" Sylvie replied, twirling a teaspoon in her coffee.

***

"I'll be in shortly," Gus called to Dee from the kitchen. He sat with his sister going over the day's events. Dee had kissed him goodnight and sleepily headed for the bedroom, a slight cant to her step.

"I just got a text from Sam," Gus whispered, showing his sister the text. "BJ has a great idea. He suggested we get the Montana family and the ladies at the ranch to stand at different coordinates. We then send Dee on a treasure type of hunt from one place to another."

"And you'll be waiting at the last coordinates with the ring," Terri grinned, her eyes rimmed with tiredness.

"And roses," Gus chuckled. "I still need to pick out a ring. Can you keep Dee busy tomorrow?"

"No problem-o, bro. We'll have a girl's day out and get to know each other," Terri winked. It was a funny lopsided wink, but Gus thought it was adorable. He loved his sister.

"Perfect," Gus replied, butterflies flapping around his insides. What if Dee said 'no'?

"Chill, Gus," Terri chuckled, folding her hand over his. "She loves you. Trust me."

His sister always could read his mind.

"I hope so," Gus croaked.

"What am I going to do with you," Terri snorted.

"With me? Nothing. With you? You're going to bed," he urged his sister.

"Probably a good idea," Terri agreed, letting go of his hand. "That was a long haul today and my back is still sore, but anything for you, little brother."

Gus and Terri stood up. He gave his sister a big hug. Emotions churned inside him. Gus wished that Emma's husband, Cleve, was still alive. He would have liked Cleve to be his best man.

"I can hear the wheels turning," Terri chuckled, pulling back from the hug.

"I know," Gus laughed. "I'm working on it. Oh, don't be frightened if someone climbs into bed with you in the middle of the night."

Gus nodded towards Dee's white muzzled Border collie lying in the middle of the floor looking expectantly up at them.

"Any time, old man," Terri said to the dog. "I'm just happy to have a bed to sleep in… a real bed…with a mattress and everything."

The collie wagged its tail and pushed itself up onto its arthritic legs. The dog followed Terri down the hall. Gus grinned until he saw the mound of dirty dishes on the counter. What happened to the kitchen he remembered cleaning only a couple of hours ago?

"Kitchen duty again," he moaned.

***

"What about Sam," Zoe asked.

"He does have a motive," Maggie agreed, eyeing Sylvie.

"Sam wouldn't hurt a fly," Sylvie snorted, raising an eyebrow.

"He would where you're concerned," Mary interjected, "but murder isn't his style. He'd whoop a man good, knock him down. In the old days, Sam was a real scrapper, but once a man was beat, Sam always walked away."

"I suppose that's the cowboy code too?" Maggie grimaced, plucking at a thread of her elegant nightgown.

"Don't you be dishing the Cowboy code," Mary rolled her eyes. "Besides, any man worth his salt stops once a man's sitting in the dirt."

"So long as he doesn't get up again," Sylvie grinned.

"Pretty much," Mary shrugged.

"I bet you caused a few of those battles, didn't you?" Sylvie teased.

"I did," Mary chortled, "but never with Sam Montana."

"So, we are back to square one," Zoe grumbled.

The ladies contemplated that for a moment.

"Are you sure Cade was killed with a handgun?" Maggie asked before biting the loose thread from her nightgown's sleeve.

"I think so, but I don't really know," Sylvie replied, startled. "Why?"

"Was it a big or little hole?" Mary asked.

"Define big or little," Sylvie replied.

"A dime, a quarter, or was his head half gone?" Mary continued.

"Ooowww," Zoe cringed.

"I guess it was about the size of a nickel," Sylvie smirked.

"Handgun then," Mary nodded sagely. "That makes it personal."

"Maybe Cade really was having an online affair," Zoe declared, lifting her chin in the air. "Maybe the story we came up with the night we killed him really happened, Maggie?"

"That's assuming he didn't die that night," Sylvie mumbled.

"Which obviously he didn't, or we wouldn't be sitting here discussing it right now," Mary reminded everyone.

"I suppose it's possible, but I would have known if he was cheating on us again," Maggie snorted in disgust.

"Again?" Zoe and Mary asked.

"Oh, yes, there was Victoria the Vivacious Vixen from Boston," Sylvie grunted.

"And let's not forget Wicked Wanda from Waxahachie or Carrie the Cow from Canada," Maggie added.

"That boy got around, didn't he," Mary stuttered, her eyes widening.

"And those are only the ones we know about," Maggie spat.

Sylvie eyed her friend suspiciously. She didn't know about Carrie the Cow from Canada, or the other two, until Maggie had told her over drinks one night.

"It seems to me that whoever this other woman was, she had a husband, and maybe that husband took offence to his wife nursing a battered philanderer back to health," Mary offered.

"Or maybe there is another explanation," Maggie murmured, suddenly engrossed by the cup of coffee on the table in front of her.

Sylvie sighed heavily and rubbed her temples. The migraine thrumming behind them was increasing in intensity.

"What do you mean by that," Zoe asked when neither Sylvie nor Maggie offered an explanation.

"What Maggie means is that my husband liked to gamble at one time," Sylvie confessed. "He got into some serious trouble, but that was decades ago. He was cleared in the end. It was right after our daughter died so I didn't blame him. I wasn't exactly a joy to be around."

"And he promised he wouldn't do it again," Maggie hissed, her eyes meeting Sylvie's.

Sylvie reached out a hand. Maggie took it in hers. Maggie smiled sadly and then let go, the pain of her betrayal not forgotten, but forgiven. It had been hard to let go, but when Maggie put her life on the line to sneak across the Mexican border to retrieve three million in ransom money to save Sylvie's and Mary's life after they were kidnapped, it was time to forgive and forget.

"What if he did," Mary mused aloud. "What if he did start gambling again? Where would he go?"

"To the track," Maggie stated without hesitation.

Sylvie nodded in agreement. "He loved watching the ponies run in person. He was accused of race fixing."

"Wasn't there a mob connection or something?" Maggie said, glancing sideways at Sylvie. "It was so long ago."

"He did," Sylvie nodded. "I can't remember the guy's name. It was something like Wally the Weasel or Tommy the Tool."

"What's with all these crazy names?" Zoe said, throwing her hands up in the air.

"It's easier to remember," Maggie laughed.

What Sylvie couldn't remember was the last time she heard Maggie laugh so heartily. How odd that Cade's murder would lighten her mood. Now that she had time to adjust, Sylvie supposed it was a bit amusing, considering both she and Maggie had confessed to killing him. Perhaps Maggie was as relieved as she was, they hadn't killed Cade.

"I think we should look into it," Mary said, looking around the table for agreement. "You know, put on our sleuthing hats."

"Like Sherlock Holmes and Watson," Zoe piped in.

"Cagney and Lacey," Sylvie said.

"Matlock and McCloud," Mary agreed.

"Tell me we won't have to follow the cowboy code," Maggie grinned evilly.

"Of course we do, we live at *The Silver Spurs Home for Aging Cowgirls*," Mary chimed.

"But you're the only cowgirl sitting at this table," Sylvie smiled. "And I want to know where my husband has been these last two years."

"So do I," Maggie smirked, raising her coffee cup like a champagne glass.

The ladies clinked coffee mugs.

"I'm glad to see you're all taking this civilly," Sam marveled as he walked into the kitchen.

"What are you toasting," Emma added breathlessly.

"We're toasting Cade," Maggie lied smoothly.

"To Cade," Mary squawked.

"To Cade," the ladies responded, banging their coffee cups together in a jaunty toast.

Sam's eyebrows creased together.

Sylvie knew he didn't believe them.

What Sam didn't know wouldn't hurt him, Sylvie told herself. If she was Catholic, Sylvie would have crossed herself. The dice had been cast. The ladies were on a mission, and they weren't going to stop until they discovered what happened to Cade after she and Maggie killed him the first time.

Chapter Ten

Been there...Jumped that!

Cole sat in his office drinking his morning cup of coffee. It was sweet, black and strong, just the way he liked it. It had been a late night and his eyes were scratchy from tiredness. The computer screen flickered in front of him. He scowled as he read the report.

Cade O'Hara's birth date, driver's license number, health information, and previous record came up on the screen in three different panels. Cole clicked on the police database files.

Thirty years previously, Cade had been charged with fraud. He was accused of fixing two races at Woodbine. The charges were dismissed, but no reason was given. That was odd. Cole googled the jockeys whose names were listed in the file. They had both been disbarred from racing that same year. That item spoke volumes – the racetrack probably didn't want the bad publicity. From then on Cade had been clean with not so much as a speeding ticket.

Cade's home address on his driver's license was the O'Hara's previous address. He hadn't changed it when the couple moved to the Montana's ranch. His health coverage had expired. There were no records of a cell phone and his tax records stopped two years ago. He also apparently didn't have a credit card.

Was he still using a card in his wife's name? Cole made a mental note to ask Mrs O'Hara.

"Where have you been the last two years," Cole murmured into his coffee cup.

His desk telephone rang. Cole absently picked up the phone.

"Cole, its Sylvie O'Hara," said the husky woman's voice on the telephone.

Speak of the devil, Cole thought.

"Mrs O'Hara, I was just about to call you."

"Well, I'm happy to save you the trouble," Mrs O'Hara replied. "I checked the horse trailer this morning and I found Cade's rain slicker and his winter coat. There are some hairs on the collar of both. Will that do?"

"Yes, definitely," Cole said, sitting forward in his chair. "I'll be right over to pick them up."

"Okay," the old woman sighed heavily.

Cole felt for her. He never really believed she killed her husband in the first place. Mrs O'Hara wasn't cold blooded enough; tough, yes, but not an icy cool-headed killer. Then again, Cole reasoned, there were lots of women in prison for murder who seemed like nice gals too.

"I need to ask," Cole continued. "Did your husband have his own credit card or bank card or does he use yours? Also, have you noticed any odd charges on yours in the last two years?"

"All of our accounts were joint," Sylvie replied thoughtfully. "I check my bank statements monthly and I would have noticed anything strange. So far, there has been nothing. Why do you ask?"

"Just dotting the 'I's' and crossing the 'T's'," Cole responded casually. "Thanks again and I'll be over in about half an hour to pick up those jackets."

Cole hung up the phone, his mind whirring.

What had Cade been living on these past two years? Had someone been supporting him?

The DNA evidence from inside the car and on his clothes hadn't been processed yet. They had found several long blond and brunette hairs on the passenger seat as well as a lot of horsehair. The horsehair was a mixed bag of silver, white, bay and chestnut. It appeared Cade had stayed true to form – being around horses was second nature to him.

Cole pushed away from his desk. He grabbed his Stetson off the coat rack and put it on.

"Sam," he called to his dispatcher as he left his inner office. "Prepare a press release and send it out. I want Cade O'Hara's name released to the media. I'll be back in a couple of hours. I'm just heading over to the Montana's to bag some evidence."

Samantha shot him a thumb's up as she answered another series of calls.

Cole walked out of the building and into a bright end of summer morning. The air was cool and crisp, the mountains in the distance picture postcard perfect.

Gus pulled up in front of him. He was driving Dee Gallant's battered farm pick-up truck.

"Hey, Cole," Gus said, leaning out the driver's side window.

"How ya doing, Gus," Cole replied amiably, walking over to stand beside the pick-up.

"I've got a favour to ask," Gus grinned. "Don't worry its nothing serious. Well to me maybe, but not you."

"Oh," Cole responded, heat rising into his cheeks. He never could keep his feelings in check. He liked Gus Rodriquez, but favours asked by Gus tended to be on the 'iffy' side. He hadn't liked him at first, but once Gus gave up on chasing Emma, Cole had relaxed into a relatively easy-going relationship with the ATF agent.

"I'm planning on asking Dee to marry me and if she says 'yes' which I'm hoping she will, I'd like you to be my best man," Gus stuttered. "I don't have any brothers. Cleve was the closest thing to it, and well, he's gone now."

"I'd be honoured," Cole stammered, stunned by the question. "That's wonderful. I'm sure Dee will say 'yes'. You guys are great together."

"Don't tell anyone," Gus nodded happily. "It's going to be a big surprise. The Montana family and the ladies know. They're going to help me set it all up. They're the only ones other than my sister, Terri. She's going to keep Dee busy for a few hours. I'm off to the city to pick out a ring."

"Say no more," Cole agreed.

"How's the case going?" Gus asked before pulling out.

"I'm waiting on DNA evidence from the scene. It's going to take a few days," Cole replied, hitching up his bands. "Looks to me like Cade stuck to what he knows. There was horse manure on his boots and horsehair on some of his clothes. There's no trace of bank accounts anywhere or credit cards in his name which is suspicious."

"Guy was cash only, huh," Gus grunted. "If you need any help, the offer still stands."

"I'll let you know," Cole finished, stepping away from the truck. "You get done what you gotta get done. Me and Emma are there for you guys. I'll watch out for your sister too."

"You can't miss my sister," Gus laughed. "She's a wild carrot-topped preacher on a Harley wearing Elton John glasses."

Cole laughed and waved to the ATF agent as Gus pulled away from the curb.

The sheriff grinned as he marched over to his Suburban, a spring in his step. What a day! His chest swelled with pride. The last time he had been a best man was at Cleve's wedding to Emma. It was bittersweet in a way.

Maybe this was a sign?

Maybe it was time to pop the question to Emma? He needed to stop hesitating.

Cole paused as he unlocked the door to the Suburban. He loved Emma, always had, but never confessed it. Cleve had been Emma's high school sweetheart. That was why Cole had joined the NFL and left town for so many years. He hadn't come back until his mama called him to tell him Cleve had died. Cole wasn't Cleve, but he knew deep down that Cleve would be okay with him dating Emma.

Cole had to admit, the thought of life without Emma and the kids was too painful to contemplate. He was pretty sure Emma loved him, but she had never said it out loud, then again, neither had he. Saying 'I love you' couldn't be that hard, could it?

***

Albert Steele didn't look like a tax investigator. He was a tall, blond, athletic, thirty-eight-year-old diehard vegan. *What goes in comes out fifty times worse* was his motto. He supported the Sierra Club and numerous animal charity and rescue organizations. It wasn't that he was a zealot or Save the Planet fanatic, but he was a passionate man.

Michael Moore's documentaries had ensured that he would forgo meat for the rest of his life.

The only thing that really angered him was tax evaders.

Tax evaders were the scum of the earth. Without taxes, there would be no roads, no hospitals, no law, and even less civility. Politically, he neither voted for one party nor the other. He disdained them all.

When the red flag appeared on the computer screen, flagging the death notice for Cade O'Hara, Albert was surprised. Coincidence or the Universe in action, Albert wasn't sure?

Cade O'Hara had won big on a long shot horse. The track had not held back the standard withholding tax. The winnings had been cashed by a name associated with a dubious organization, After Eight Incorporated, a company that had also been flagged by the tax bureau for its connections to organized crime. Further investigation revealed that Cade O'Hara hadn't filed a tax return for the past two years.

Albert tapped away at his keyboard until he found the details he wanted.

Cade O'Hara's death had been reported by a sheriff in a hick town in the mountains. The local coroner's office listed the manner of death as murder. The words 'Active Investigation' came up on his screen.

Albert opened the file on his desk and looked at the information within. Mrs Sylvie O'Hara was still alive. She lived near the sheriff's office that filed the press release. Mrs O'Hara's marital status on her last tax return was 'Separated'. Accompanying the tax form was a court notice that an 'Order of Substituted Service' had been filed because her husband couldn't be found. Separated wasn't divorced. The final divorce was still pending.

Albert grinned. A trip to the mountains was in order.

***

Gus had just pulled up in front of Friedman's Jewellery store when his cell phone dinged. He parked the truck and then tapped on the screen, opening the message from his partner at the office.

'Your pal O'Hara won half a million bucks on a long shot and cashed the cheque with a guy associated with a mob bookie named Johnny Brillio. There's an open fraud investigation with the Western and Eastern offices involving three more suspected racing 'fixes' at three different racetracks. Head office has been informed that you are in the area and acquainted with local law enforcement. Expect a call. Vacation's over, or extended, depending on how you look at it. What have you gotten yourself into up there?'

"Damn," Gus swore, typing out a response.

'Email me the files. Let me know how much I can tell the local sheriff. P.S. Going to ask her to marry me.'

'Good luck, man,' was the response.

Gus slammed his hands angrily down on the steering wheel. He did not want to be involved in this.

***

"You know, Gus' sister is a pastor, Sylvie," Emma said from her place at the table. Sam and the kids and Zoe were out in the barn. Cole had already been and gone. "I bet she would be happy to conduct the ceremony."

"I don't know," Sylvie huffed. "There're only me and you guys. Maybe we can simply toast the old geezer here afterwards."

"True, we could," Maggie agreed.

Sylvie looked questioningly at her friend.

"Let's face it, most of our friends are dead, Sylvie," Maggie replied simply, none of her characteristic crustiness evident. "The rest of the hunt club haven't even bothered to write or email us. I haven't received one Christmas card since we left the coast, have you?"

Sylvie decided not to tell Maggie about the oodles of Christmas cards she received every year, including the past two. She had secreted them away in her room. What was the point? Inflict more pain? Remind Maggie of the obvert racism she had endured over the years? To be honest, most of it wasn't from the riders or trainers or the host organizations, it was the bone-headed public.

Maggie didn't make friends easily. People bluntly asked Sylvie why she bothered? Why hadn't she tossed Maggie to the curb years ago? Everyone knew about Cade and Maggie's affair. It was the worst kept secret in the world. Sometimes even Sylvie wondered why, and then Maggie would do something outrageous like risk her life to save her or spend all night walking her stallion in subzero temperatures after Buddy colicked at the last horse show he was in. Maggie had also helped nurse her back to health both during and after chemo. Maggie Carroll was the worst and the best friend a person could ever have.

"I agree with Emma. We should still have a eulogy at the funeral service," Mary urged her. "The closure would do you good."

"Oh, I closed that book already," Sylvie smirked.

Maggie stared into her coffee cup. She looked thoughtful. Sylvie idly wondered if she was remembering Cade or wondering who he was sleeping with?

"Why don't I ask Gus to ask his sister if she will do it first," Emma insisted. "We can decide from there."

"You aren't going to leave this alone, are you?" Sylvie snorted.

"No, I'm not," Emma grinned.

"And neither am I," agreed Mary.

"Okay, call Gus," Sylvie agreed. "The office manager at the church told me this morning that there is an opening this Saturday at one. Cole told me before he left that he'll release the body. Cade always wanted to be buried with one of those lifelines from the coffin to a bell above the ground so that he could ring it in case he was buried alive. Cremation was out of the question."

"He had nightmares about going to Hell," Maggie whispered.

"Hmmmhmmn," Sylvie replied, her eyes narrowing. "That's because he probably is."

"Well, this is getting depressing," Mary scolded the crew. "It's five o'clock somewhere. Let's have a shot of Bailey's and toast the crazy so-and-so."

"We did that last night," Maggie replied disapprovingly.

"So, we'll do it again," Sylvie declared, smacking a hand on the table.

"Not for me," Emma waved, standing up. "I'm going to join the kids. They're riding into the hills in an hour to start mapping out the places for Gus' whacky proposal."

"That sounds like fun," Mary chuckled, retrieving the bottle of Irish cream from the liquor cabinet in the corner.

"Wait a minute, weren't they bringing down the cows today?"

"They were, but the cows came down by themselves much to Jenny's disappointment."

"Oooh, is it that time already," Zoe asked, wandering into the room, her face sun-kissed and eyes bright with anticipation.

"It is now," Mary laughed, plunking the bottle on the table.

"I'm out of here," Emma chuckled, racing for the door.

"What are we toasting?" Zoe purred.

"Cade," Maggie informed her.

"Didn't we do that already?" Zoe repeated, puzzled.

"Yes," Sylvie snapped.

"And then we're going to start asking more pointed questions of the sheriff," Maggie declared suddenly, sitting up straighter. "After that, you and I, Sylvie, are going to start making some calls to those 'friends' we don't hear from anymore. I am sure somebody knows something about where Cade has been and who he has been involved with for the last two years. This is the age of social media. There is no such thing as anonymous anymore."

Sylvie grinned. There was the Maggie she knew and loved.

Chapter Eleven

Leave a horse's gate unfastened and he'll be knocking on your window in the night.

The ladies sat at the table with Emma and Sam as they did every night after the dinner dishes were cleared, chatting about the day's events or sharing horse stories from the past. Tonight, they had a handmade map laid out on the table with nine locations marked with a gold star from one of Jenny's home school projects on it. Each gold star represented a spot where one of them would wait for Dee, hand her a red rose (Jenny's idea), and then a note with the coordinates to the next checkpoint. Jenny's name was beside the first checkpoint by the swimming hole. BJ's name was at the second location, close to his sister, and everyone else was now picking theirs.

BJ had already excused himself and gone out to the barn to brush the colt, leaving Zoe and Maggie to fight over who had the last checkpoint before the spot in the canyon where Tommy Cortez had been found.

"Why don't you rock, paper, scissors it," Sylvie suggested, "or we'll be here all night."

"I am not leaving it to chance," Zoe argued.

"Me neither," Maggie agreed, glaring at Zoe.

Sam rolled his eyes. The pair had been arguing for over an hour now. Emma, Sylvie and Mary all looked amused.

"I was the one Tommy asked to marry him so it should be me in the spot immediately before the canyon," Zoe ranted for the umpteenth time.

"But you didn't marry him, did you," Maggie retorted, also for the umpteenth time.

"I've had enough," Sam growled, leaning forward menacingly. "I'm calling Dee's mother and father. They are going to be in that spot. I'll stay back with Jenny to make sure she doesn't get into any trouble. I've made my decision and that is the end of it!"

If Superman's laser eyesight was real, Sam knew he would be dead right now. At least Maggie and Zoe were wise enough to bite back any remarks. Thank heavens for small mercies, Sam fumed.

"Grandpa, mom, Sylvie, you better come see this," Jenny yelled from the living room.

"What is it," Emma called, not budging from the table.

"Cade is on TV," the little girl hollered back.

"That's impossible!" Sylvie started.

Everyone rushed into the living room. They took various seats around the room, eyes fixed on the sixty-inch television Sam had purchased last year, Sylvie and Emma flanking Jenny on the couch, Sam in is Lazy Boy, and Zoe and Maggie sitting separately on winged back chairs.

"Cade O'Hara, pictured here with his wife, Sylvie O'Hara, at the Madison Square Gardens Horse Show twelve years ago," the News anchor was saying, "was found dead two days ago, shot execution style in the head, after winning five hundred thousand dollars during the recent Del Mar's Thoroughbred Club Derby weekend, after the longshot, One Flashy Dame, beat the favorite, Steam Train, by a nose. We go live to Stacy Lindsay who is with Sheriff Cole Trane on site in the Rocky Mountains."

"Half a million dollars," Emma gasped.

"That's a lot of money, isn't it," Jenny asked innocently.

"Yeah," Emma nodded, wide eyed.

"Guess we know what he was doing," Sylvie spat, she and Maggie exchanging a furious look.

"And where he's been," Maggie snarled.

The television closed in on a pretty brunette in a navy-blue suit outside of Cole's office. Cole stood, hat in hand, looking comfortable and official in front of the camera. Sam was glad it was Cole and not one of Cole's deputies blundering about. Cole was used to cameras and media.

"Thank you, Brian," Stacy said with a somber voice. "Of course, everyone remembers you as *The Cole Train* from your wide receiver days in the NFL, but I don't think folks expected you to become a sheriff after Sammy Daws leveled you in the Super Bowl, Cole."

Sam chuckled. The girl was obviously trying to ruffle Cole, but the only person that could get under Cole's skin was Sam's daughter-in-law.

"That's right, Stacy, I ran for sheriff about a year after I left the NFL," Cole smiled. "This is my hometown. Folks believe in me here. I'm honored to serve."

"Let's hope they believe you can find the person responsible for murdering Cade O'Hara," the reporter replied smoothly, and then changed directions. "You were also responsible for aiding in the capture of America's most wanted felon, Tommy Cortez, two years ago, is that right?"

"I did, and there is no doubt in my mind that we'll catch Mr O'Hara's killer," Cole responded, staring fixedly into the camera. *"The Cole Train* isn't done yet. I may have a different team working for me now, but they are committed, smart and just as determined as any NFL-er."

"Good for you," Emma whooped. "Go get her, babe!"

"Yay, Cole," Jenny cheered, not really understanding why, but her mother was doing it.

Sylvie and Sam grinned.

"Do you think this was a mob hit, sheriff?" Stacy purred, stepping closer to Cole.

"You don't need to hear this," Sylvie rumbled, placing her hands over Jenny's ears.

"I mean, come on, this guy wins a half a million bucks and then ends up with a bullet hole in his head. If that doesn't spell organized crime, nothing does," the lady shark continued.

Cole leaned forward to speak directly into the reporter's microphone, totally unruffled.

"I have no comment on the case at this time, Stacy," Cole nodded slightly. "It is an active investigation. When I have more information to report, you'll be the one I call."

Cole smiled into the camera, put on his cowboy hat, and ambled back towards his office seemingly without a care in the world: interview over.

Sam slapped his knee.

"Wait!" the reporter yelled, racing after him. "Is his wife a suspect? I heard he was quite the womanizer. Was this a crime of passion?"

Cole waggled his fingers at the news reporter before disappearing into the office, closing the door firmly behind him.

"That hussy," Zoe hissed.

"I can think of a better word than that," Sylvie snapped.

"So can I," Maggie fumed.

"Cole already questioned us," Zoe sniffed. "We were all together when Cade was killed."

"Grandpa," BJ yelled, barging through the front door and into the living room. "There's a whole bunch of cars and vans screaming up the lane!"

Sam leapt out of his chair. He strode quickly towards the gun cabinet and took down a shotgun. He loaded it with buckshot and headed for the door.

"Sam don't do anything stupid," Sylvie warned him. "I can handle anything those bozos throw at me."

"What's going on," Jenny cried, whipping Sylvie's hands from over her ears.

"Go upstairs, Jenny," Emma commanded. "BJ go with her and keep your faces away from the window. I don't want those new crews to see you."

"But I want to help grandpa," the teen argued.

"The best help you can be is making sure your sister stays in her bedroom," Sam said to the boy, his pointed look garnering a quick response.

BJ hustled his tearful sister up the stairs.

"Call Cole," Sam barked at Emma.

Emma ran for the phone.

"You ladies stay in the house," Sam turned towards the women as he popped the shotgun case closed. "No arguments from you either."

The news crews screeched to a halt in front of the house.

"You know if Cade wasn't already dead, I could kill him again," Maggie sneered.

"I hear you, sister," Sylvie muttered.

"Cole and his deputies are on the way," Emma said to Sam, and then to the ladies: "I put water on for tea. It might be more calming under the circumstances."

The lights from a barrage of different news crews lit up the front room.

Sam took a deep breath and opened the door, keeping the shotgun lowered, his face blank. He didn't want anyone to think he was a threat, but also wanted to make a statement" nobody was getting past him and they were trespassing on private property.

"Y'all get off my property," he growled, stepping onto the porch.

Lights instantly blinded him.

Microphones were stuffed in his face.

"Did you kill Cade O'Hara?" a reporter asked pointedly, bravely tapping his microphone on the end of the shotgun.

Bulldozer and Dozer Junior picked that moment to barrel out of the barn and across the yard, knocking cameras and camera crews flying. Curses and surprised shouts rang through the air.

Bulldozer leapt at the young reporter who had his microphone closest to Sam's face. The hundred-and-fifty-pound Saint Bernard wrapped her jaws around the foam ball atop the mic and bit down. There was a large crunching sound.

"Your dog ate my mic," the reporter screamed.

"She'll eat more than that if you don't get out of my face," Sam chortled.

"I'll sue," the man stammered, the back of his hand and what was left of the microphone dripping with drool.

Dozer Junior exuberantly jumped up on the next nearest reporter, his tail wagging furiously. The young dog was having a great time.

"You go right ahead," Sam replied, his anger dissipating. Foam microphone balls were bouncing off the ground everywhere as the dogs mowed down more and more reporters. The camera men had the sense to jump back into their vehicles and roll up the windows.

"Like I said, this is private property," Sam nodded, lifting the shotgun so that the muzzle stood upright facing the porch roof. It was mostly for show, but, if necessary, he was prepared to blast a van with buckshot.

"There ain't a judge around here would convict me," Sam hollered after the retreating news crews.

Maybe he'd been around the women too long? The ladies no-nonsense don't-mess-with-me attitude was wearing off on him.

Red, white and blue lights appeared on the highway. He could hear the sirens before Cole and his deputies arrived in force. Dee's pickup truck roared into the lane from the other direction.

***

Cole stood alongside Gus, Emma and Sam on the porch. One of his deputies was stationed at the far gate leading into the ranch. He had sent the rest home after the last of the news people had been run off. The two Saint Bernards lay on the porch snoozing. They were exhausted. The pair had channeled their inner Border collie, corralling two of the more stubborn reporters in the barn. The reporters thought they could hide until the law was gone. Darned fools were lucky one of the studs didn't lay into them.

Cole rubbed his eyes. It had been a long day and he was bone weary. An arm wrapped itself around his waist. He smiled down at Emma. Her eyes shone with gratitude and warmth.

"You know I was thinking," Gus spoke, his voice deep and resonant.

"That's a dangerous thing coming from you," Sam kidded, the shotgun tucked safely under one arm, the barrel open, the shells removed.

Gus grinned.

"I was thinking on a question that pretty reporter didn't shout at you when you were running away from her and she was charging after you," Gus chuckled.

"Cole wasn't running away, he had finished the interview," Emma scolded Gus. "Isn't that right Cole?"

"Yes, Em, you are correct," Cole smirked, hugging her close. "And I know where you're going with this, Gus."

"Where's the money?" Gus explained. "Cade won all that cash, bought a sweet little Mercedes, some new clothes, and headed out on the road, but where did all the race winnings go?"

"I know, I've been asking myself that same question," Cole agreed. "I'm hoping the press release and the media free-for-all will shake some trees and we get some calls."

"Now that we're involved, I thought I'd give the lab a call and ask them to put a rush on the DNA evidence you sent off," Gus nodded.

Emma leaned her head against his shoulder. It felt good, Cole had to admit.

"I'd appreciate it," Cole acknowledged huskily.

Sam suppressed a grin. Cole caught it and smiled back.

"On a happier note," Emma broke in, "when do you want to do the proposal? BJ and Jenny worked it all out and the ladies have finally stopped arguing about where they are going to be."

"After I put my foot down," Sam laughed heartily. "I thought we'd get Dee's parents involved. Dee's going to know something's up after she finds me and Jenny at the first coordinates."

"That's a great idea," Gus agreed, blushing. "I talked to her father yesterday on my way back from getting the ring. He gave me his heartfelt approval to ask for his daughter's hand in marriage."

"Oh, speaking of which, you want me to release your girls now," Cole chimed.

"Yeah, I think they've learned their lesson," Gus blushed.

"Dee is in jail?" Emma gasped, slapping Cole on the arm.

"Hey, don't blame me, Gus wanted me to jail her."

"And my sister," Gus nodded.

"Now what did those two hooligans get up to that warranted a night in jail?" Sam marveled.

"Where do I begin," Cole lamented.

"Oh, I don't know, the wet t-shirt contest at the biker bar or popping wheelies down Main Street?" Gus snorted.

"Or we cut straight to the chase," Cole tipped his hat forward. "They flashed my deputies and then went skinny dipping in the fountain outside of Jay Henry's place."

"That sister of yours is a pistol, ain't she," Sam guffawed.

"She is that," Gus moaned. "I'll go pick them up. We can put Terri's Harley in the back of the truck."

"Should we be getting your sister to perform the eulogy for Cade on Saturday?" Emma queried; her brows creased with worry.

"Don't worry, she'll be fine," Gus said. "Terri hasn't been on home soil for five years. She needed to blow off some steam."

"Come on, Emma, let's let these boys go about their business," Sam chortled. "Cole looks like he's about to fall over and Gus...well, either Dee's going to be contrite or angrier than a freshly knockered bull."

Emma snorted with amusement. The men laughed. Emma then stood on her tiptoes and kissed Cole on the cheek. Cole felt his cheeks redden.

Sam nodded his good-byes and went into the house. Gus winked at Emma and leapt off the porch before jumping into his truck and speeding down the drive. He turned left instead of right at the end of the lane, heading for town.

Cole wrapped his arms around Emma and kissed her passionately. Her lips were moist and willing.

"You take care of yourself," Emma murmured breathlessly.

"I will," he replied.

"Promise me you'll let Gus and his men take down any mob guys if it comes to that," she sobbed.

"Oh, honey, I promise I won't take any unnecessary chances," he consoled her, hugging her close, his heart breaking at the thought of her worrying about him; although, he had to confess a tiny bit of him was thrilled by the idea.

"Okay," she sniffled.

He kissed her once more.

***

"Ouch," Sylvie cried, stumbling backwards as the door slammed into her shoulder.

"What were you doing skulking around behind a closed door," Sam grinned, closing said door behind him.

"I wasn't skulking," she argued. "I was just about to ask if you wanted anything to drink out there."

"Sure, you were."

Mary, Zoe, and Maggie peeked out at him from the kitchen.

"And that goes for you three as well," Sam rumbled, wagging a finger at them.

"What was that about money?" Sylvie wheedled, following Sam to the gun cabinet.

"I guess they haven't found the race winnings yet," Sam informed the woman at his back. He put the shotgun away, placed the two unused shells back in the box, and then locked up the cabinet, tucking the key inside his shirt pocket. When he turned around, all four women circled him. They looked like a pack of hyenas out for blood.

"Now, don't you gals get your knickers in a twist over this," he warned them. "Let the professionals handle it. I know you lot. Gus and Cole will find the missing cash and hunt down the killer responsible for murdering Cade."

The women smirked at him; their faces set stubbornly in a 'you can't tell us what to do' look. Sam rolled his shoulders back and shrugged away the stiffness in his back.

"The press is gone, the sheriff is leaving shortly, and the horses, dogs and kids are bedded down for the night," Sam replied gruffly. "I'm going to bed. I suggest you lot mosey on off to your own bedrooms and stop hatching any more plans that might get you thrown in jail."

"Party pooper," Mary chirped, heading for the stairs.

"Killjoy," Zoe quipped, wiggling her fanny and her fingers at the same time.

Lord, save me, Sam grimaced.

Maggie shot him her characteristic glare and followed the women up the stairs to their bedrooms.

"And what about you," Sam asked Sylvie.

"Are Gus' sister and Dee really in jail for flashing and skinny dipping in a fountain?" Sylvie whispered, looking around first to make sure the ladies didn't hear.

"Looks like it," Sam chuckled, the stress of the day catching up to him.

"Wish I was there," Sylvie purred, swatting him playfully on the behind.

"I bet you do," he mumbled back.

Sam escorted Sylvie to her bedroom door.

"You know, I am a widow now," she teased him, giving him a sexy come-hither look, before quickly ducking into her bedroom and slamming the door in his face.

He should have expected that. The vixen!

Sam grinned and pushed open the door next to Sylvie's. That look she gave him was going to keep him awake all night.

Chapter Twelve

The hardest thing about learning to ride is the ground.

Cole's deputies kept the line of media vans and reporters at bay as Pastor Scallon spoke softly about Cade's life, his passion for horses, and his love for the two women in his life, his wife and his long-term mistress. Sylvie had insisted upon it. Maggie's iron exterior had finally collapsed under the weight of Sylvie's forgiveness and compassion. Cade's other indiscretions were left unspoken. Even Zoe held her tongue, exhibiting a quiet dignity.

Sylvie and Maggie stood side by side in their grief, neither crying nor wailing, each lost in their own thoughts. Sam looked on, his eyes hooded, from his place three steps away from Sylvie. Mary and Zoe flanked the wiry senior cowboy.

Cole, Emma, Gus, and Dee, were on the far side of the casket, Cole and Gus standing shoulder to shoulder, scanning the crowd. It was larger than anyone anticipated.

Cole recognized several of the townsfolk including all of the staff of the local bar and dance hall frequented, plus the feed store owner and a couple of his staff, Nan and the bank manager of the only bank in town. He wondered if the bank manager was there to pay his condolences or hoping that Sylvie would be adding a half million dollars to her portfolio. The media circus had inspired a lot of out-of-town attendees as well. So far, the crowd was respectful and manageable, but Cole knew that could change in an instant.

There were three men present that intrigued him. Two of them wore expensive navy pinstripe suits, totally out of place in Cole's small town. They looked to be related. The third man was tall and athletic. He wore an off the rack grey blazer with a thin black tie and white shirt underneath. Crisp black jeans completed the package. Cole elbowed Gus.

"Already on it," Gus whispered, discreetly snapping a picture of the two men with his cell phone and messaging it off to his partner.

"Cade is gone now from this earthly dwelling and has left behind those who mourn his absence. Grant that we may hold his memory dear, never bitter for what we have lost nor in regret for the past, but always in hope of the eternal kingdom where you will bring us together again," Terri stated, completing the ceremony. "Amen."

"Amen," the mourners murmured.

"You're not going to believe this," Gus said, leaning into Cole. "My partner recognized one of the two pinstripes. He's a henchman for a Chicago loan shark that dabbles in firearms and Indian tobacco smuggling."

"What about the blond?" Cole whispered back.

"What blond?"

"The guy in the grey blazer with the bulging muscles," Cole nodded.

Gus snapped a quick picture of Albert Steele and sent it off for identification.

"Do you two ever stop working," Emma hissed as Sylvie and Maggie approached the pastor.

Cole shrugged helplessly.

"That was a lovely ceremony," Dee sniffed, dabbing at her eyes.

"It was, wasn't it?" Emma agreed, embracing Dee.

"Why don't you girls go join my sister and the ladies," Gus insisted.

"While we go have a chat with those two guys over there," Cole nodded towards the best dressed men at the funeral. "And don't worry, Em, no fireworks, I promise."

"There better not be," Emma growled, hooking an arm under Dee's.

The two women headed off to join the Sylvie and her clan now chatting with Terri.

The two henchmen looked around, distinctly uncomfortable at the news crews scattered about, cameras whirring. They unsuccessfully tried to hide their faces.

"Those suits are tailored, think they're carrying," Cole asked the ATF agent.

"I do," Gus acknowledged as he and Cole casually sauntered towards the pretty news reporter Cole had run from a few days earlier.

At the last minute, they turned towards the taller of the two men. The mob enforcer saw them and did a quick about face, heading towards the crowd at a fast walk, his partner glued to his side.

Cole and Gus increased their pursuit.

"Follow them," Stacy ordered her cameraman.

***

Albert Steele grinned. He couldn't wait to confront the recently widowed Sylvie O'Hara. She didn't look like the grieving sort. He noticed she hadn't cried once throughout the monotonous ceremony. She wore a black silk blazer over an ankle length grey cotton dress. Her silver-streaked dark red hair was swept up in a tight coif. She was regal looking, he had to admit.

The tall, bronzed woman with a mane of black hair cascading down the back of her ebony pant suit standing beside his quarry reminded him of Cher. She was stunning in her beauty, despite her age, and carried herself with a casual elegance.

Albert smiled as he walked by the other two old ladies and the cowboy gathered around the preacher, barely paying them any heed. He slowly pulled the tax notice from inside his left blazer pocket.

"I'm sorry for your loss, Mrs O'Hara," he told her, sounding as sympathetic as possible. Sylvie turned towards him. Her steely gaze pierced his resolve.

"Funny, you don't sound very sorry," the woman remarked dryly.

For a moment, Albert was speechless.

"Did you know my husband well?" she asked suspiciously.

Of course, Albert reasoned, she thought he was a reporter.

"Not really," he said truthfully, contrite even, "but I do know he owes the government a substantial sum."

Albert slipped the tax notice letter into her hand.

"As his wife and sole heir, you will be responsible for paying it," Albert smiled. "Sorry to be the bearer of bad tidings at a time like this."

Gosh but he loved his job.

"Is that so," Sylvie sneered.

Albert had but a minute to realize that Sylvie O'Hara and her friends were not like any of the frail old ladies or grieving families he had personally delivered tax notices to in the past. He should have done his research.

***

Pandemonium erupted.

The news crews broke through Cole's line of deputies like Moses parting the Red Sea. The funeral onlookers raised their fists and seethed towards the grave site en masse.

Cole and Gus lost sight of the two men they were chasing as they were carried back towards the gravesite by the crowd.

Gus turned around and saw the tall blond man Cole had pointed out lying on the ground, arms covering his face, as Sylvie O'Hara, Maggie Carroll, Zoe Puddicombe, Mary Adams, and his sister, pummelled the man with fists and boots. In his sister's case, she was whacking him over the head with a bible. Sam Montana was valiantly trying to haul Sylvie off the man, but Sylvie spun around and socked him in the jaw, and then went back to kicking the prone man with a pointy toed boot. Emma and Dee while not in the fray, cheered the ladies on. Cade's coffin was rocking on its stand.

As Cole ran past him, racing to save the poor soul on the ground's life, Gus wondered how on earth he was going to propose to Dee tomorrow if everyone involved in his plan was in jail.

Chapter Thirteen

Save a horse, ride a cowboy

Gus paced back and forth inside the rocky canyon where Tommy Cortez, notorious coyote and drug smuggler, had fallen and broken his leg after his plane crashed farther up the mountain. This was the exact spot where Gus fell in love with Ranger Dee Gallant.

Dee's parents had happily supplied the raw-boned appaloosa he had ridden in on. It was a cantankerous pot-bellied beast, a red roan with a white blanket, and a wispy mane and tail. He fervently wished to be back aboard Sunny, Dee's bay Quarter horse.

As he paced, Gus rehearsed his lines as he rolled the engagement ring, a hexagonal diamond with two smaller ones on either side, around and around on his pinkie finger.

"You are my everything. I would die if I had to live without you," he said to the horse. "No, she'd think I'm suicidal."

The horse pinned back its ears and angrily swished its tail.

"I see you agree with me. How about 'you are the sun at the center of my galaxy'," he croaked. "Ugh, how corny is that?"

Gus struggled to concentrate.

It was hot in the canyon, not scorching summer hot, but enough to wilt the dozen roses he held tightly in one hand.

Gus let out a long-frustrated sigh. He was lucky today was even happening. The ladies from *The Silver Spurs Home for Aging Cowgirls* had spent the night in jail, as had his sister... again... for the assault on the government tax assessor. The assessor, Albert Steele, wanted to press charges, but Cole had convinced the lady reporter that a tax collector going after a poor elderly grieving widow at her husband's funeral was a better story than four old ladies and one preacher laying a beat-down on the man. Steele's superior had the assault charges dropped by morning after the global news media picked up the story. What a fiasco though.

Gus heard the clip-clop of horse's hooves and strode out into the middle of the arroyo, his stomach twisted into knots. It was time.

He brushed his hair back with one hand, almost forgetting the engagement ring on his finger, and then fumbled to get it off. With a groan, he wrenched the ring off his pinkie, tucked it inside his shirt pocket and waited for Dee to arrive.

A buckskin horse with a handsome long haired woman on board jogged up the canyon.

Gus let out a sigh: it was Dee's mother.

"Relax, honey, I just wanted to bring you a cold lemonade and some lunch," Mrs Gallant chuckled, reaching into her saddle bags and pulling out a can of lemonade and a roast beef sandwich. "We can't have you passing out from thirst or hunger."

"Thanks, Mrs Gallant, I'm not sure I could eat right now, but the drink is appreciated," Gus replied, reaching for the ice ringed lemonade. How the woman had kept the drink cold was beyond Gus, but he was grateful.

"Not surprised," she grinned. "Don't worry, it will all work out."

"I hope so," he stammered.

Dee's mother laughed lightly. She was a stunning woman with long salt and pepper hair, tanned skin, and laugh lines that crinkled merrily when she laughed. If girls looked like their mothers when they got older, Gus was going to be a lucky man.

***

Sam sat on a rock rubbing his sore chin while Jenny tossed pebbles into the quicksilver lake. The lake's surface was as smooth as glass. He tugged down the lip of his Stetson to shade his eyes from the midday sun.

It was hotter than at the funeral yesterday. The Farmer's Almanac so far was way off base – winter couldn't come soon enough.

Despite everything, Sam had to smile. Sylvie sure was a cracker. While Sylvie had long suffered her cheating husband, apparently it was open season on bandits and tax collectors. Not for the first time Sam wondered what hold the crab apple haired woman had over him.

Steel hit rock.

"Here she comes, Jenny," Sam warned his granddaughter.

Jenny grinned, dropping her handful of pebbles into the lake. She quickly wiped her hands on her jeans, and then slipped the note out of her back pocket and retrieved the rose from the shade of a bush where she had left it.

Sam had to hand it to his granddaughter, she was organized. He vowed to pencil this day on the calendar. It didn't happen very often.

Sam leapt off the rock and jogged over to stand beside Jenny on the small sandy beach, placing one arm on her shoulder to steady her. She may have had the important stuff in hand, but her little body was vibrating with excitement.

Sam's paint mare and Jenny's pony whinnied a greeting to the rugged bay mustang as Dee trotted out of the bush.

"What are you two doing here," Dee gasped, reining in the mustang.

Sam almost laughed at the dazed look on her face and the brown bow tied cardboard box resting against one hip.

"Ranger Dee, you have been served," Jenny piped up, a look as serious as a court bailiff on her freckled face as she stepped forward and handed Dee first the rose and then the note with the new coordinates on it.

"I'll take that," Sam said, reaching for the cardboard box.

"But, where's the hawk?" Dee stammered, fumbling with the piece of paper, rose, and box.

Sam relieved the ranger of the box.

"I don't get it, its coordinates," Dee mumbled, still confused.

"You will," Sam grinned.

"Better hurry," Jenny advised her, "your rose is dying."

Dee shook her head in consternation and turned her mount around. She glanced at the coordinates typed out on the sheet of paper, and then back over her shoulder at Sam and Jenny.

Sam and Jenny waved good-bye.

"Okay, message Zoe she's on her way," Sam instructed his granddaughter. "She's next, right?"

"Right," Jenny nodded, pulling out the family's one cell phone.

"Come on, kiddo, let's mount up," Sam grinned after Jenny sent the message.

"This is fun," Jenny chirruped, bouncing up and down like a basketball at a Harlem Globetrotter's game.

"It is, isn't it," Sam agreed.

***

Sweat poured off Dee's forehead and pooled under her armpits as she leaned forward so the rugged eggbeater of a mustang could more easily climb the shale slope to the next coordinates.

Zoe Puddicombe, looking as cool as ever, sat atop her white stallion on top of the plateau, her black bolero hat, white tailed formal jacket, ebony riding pants, and spit polished leather riding boots, reminded Dee of pictures she'd seen in an art gallery in Mexico. Only Zoe could rock the royal blue wing tipped spiky grey hair.

Zoe grinned, her eyes dancing as she held out a folded piece of paper with yet another set of coordinates on it and another red rose.

Dee's mustang shied away from the stallion at first, but the stallion stood resolute, calm and unruffled. The gelding settled and Dee slipped the paper and rose out of Zoe's hand, adding the new rose to the other.

"What is this," Dee interrogated Zoe.

"Continue on," Zoe waved a gloved hand in dismissal. "All will be revealed."

Dee smirked and backed the gelding away from the white stallion. She reviewed the next set of coordinates. She recognized them. It was the abandoned mining town where Mary and Sylvie had been held hostage last year.

Dee let the mustang set the pace as they made their way down the mountain. The gelding's neck was wet, but he didn't appear to be suffering from the heat as much as both Dee and the two roses did.

"Okay, you guys, spill the beans," she called to the two ladies sitting in lawn chairs drinking marguerites outside the crumbling hotel with boarded up windows as she approached.

The two friends roared with laughter as they staggered to their feet. They had been there for awhile.

"For you, my dear," Sylvie replied with a sweeping courtier's gesture as she handed Dee yet another red rose.

"Indubitably," Mary snorted, handing Dee a piece of paper.

"I feel like I'm on the Bachelor or something, only you two aren't hunky Speedo clad men," Dee said, exasperated.

"Would you like a marguerita before you go," Mary asked.

"No thanks, I think I better keep my head on straight for whatever this is," Dee chuckled.

"Well, we don't have to," Sylvie shrugged. "However, there is a bucket of water for your horse over there."

"Thank you," Dee answered, noticing the truck and horse trailer tucked in the corral behind the building for the first time.

She left the ladies to return to their lawn chairs and rode over to the horse trailer. The trailer was empty but there were two buckets filled with water on the ground beside the truck.

Once the mustang had emptied the buckets and Dee had quenched her own thirst from the canteen tied to her saddle horn, Dee read the next set of bearings.

"The mine, huh?"

Dee reined the mustang around and jogged past the ladies, heading up the two-lane trail that lead to the barricaded gold mine in the hills above the mining town.

"See ya later alligator," Mary chimed.

"In a while crocodile," Sylvie giggled.

Dee laughed heartily. Whatever the Montana family and their clan were up to, she was up for it.

Dee continued to follow the trail of coordinates up the hill to where BJ waited in front of the mine; down the trail past Sylvie and Mary who were getting more and more inebriated by the minute, up the path to the ranger cabin where Maggie stood beside BJ's buckskin Quarter horse, a wide grin on her face. Dee was almost frightened by that one; she had never seen Maggie smile before. She was also relieved that Maggie's crazy chestnut stallion was nowhere to be seen. After that, it was Cole and Emma, and then back down the mountain towards the Montana ranch.

Dee was almost angry with Cole and Emma. They refused to give her so much as a hint as to what was going on. Her hands were cramping as she held the six roses tightly in one hand, the reins being in the other. The flowers' petals were starting to fall off in the heat.

Dee's back and inner thigh muscles were getting sore. Her mouth was parched, her canteen empty. The mustang was starting to drag. The two had covered at least ten miles in this crazy game her friends had set up.

It wasn't until she saw her mom and dad sitting aboard their matching pair of buckskins, roses in their hands, beatific smiles on their faces that it donned on her what was going on. Tears welled in her mother's eyes as she silently handed Dee a rose. Her father then handed her the last rose, and both her parents side stepped their horses away from each other, creating an opening for Dee to ride down the canyon.

Dee's heart thudded in her chest. The hand that held the eight roses began to tremble. Weariness sloughed off the mustang as her anxiety increased and he picked up his gait.

She rode along the narrow trail. Steep granite walls rose on either side of her, shading Dee and her horse. Gus stood at the end of the canyon. His face was as red as the dozen roses he held out towards her as he took one knee and reached into his pocket for a ring. The diamond sent rainbows of light ricocheting off the rocky slope.

"Dee Gallant, will you marry me?" he asked simply.

Dee leapt off her horse and ran to the gorgeous hunk of man kneeling in the dirt. He was better than any bachelor on TV.

"Yes," she yelled. "Yes. Yes, and yes!"

"Thank God," Gus laughed, standing up and slipping the ring onto her finger. "I was so afraid you'd say 'no'."

"You planned all this," she laughed, wrapping her arms around him.

"I had help... lots of help," Gus grinned.

The two kissed, passionately and deeply. They broke away from each other as Dee's parents cantered up behind them.

"And you guys were in on it as well," Dee chastised her parents. "How on earth did you keep this a secret?"

"It was tough, but the whole world heard you yell 'yes'," her father replied, his eyes twinkling.

"Wait a minute, someone's missing," Dee gasped, counting off her stops on her fingers. "Where's Terri?"

"On kitchen duty at the Montana's for her un-pastor like behaviour yesterday," Gus chuckled.

"There's a party waiting to happen back at the ranch," Dee's mother smiled.

"Yeah, about that. Sylvie and Mary started early. Maybe someone better go retrieve them," Dee laughed. She turned to Gus and kissed her man again. He was one bachelor who was off the market.

Chapter Fourteen

When your horse bolts for 10 minutes flat, you know to get off and give up. The question is, how?
Annarose Robinson

"Well, it's a good thing I could drive that monster truck of Sam's," Maggie smirked, clinking her champagne glass against Dee's. "There was no way I was letting Sylvie or Mary drive in their condition."

"Yes, they were quite tippled when I saw them," Dee chuckled.

"I'm glad you were driving too, Miss Maggie," BJ agreed, "especially since it was my horse in the trailer."

"Oh, sweetie, I'd never drink and drive," Sylvie told the still anxious teen. "And neither would Mary. We knew Mags would get us all home safely. She handles that big rig of mine like it's a micro-bus. Your grandpa's rig is nothing compared to that."

"Speaking of which, where is the other juvenile delinquent anyway," Sam asked, a can of Budweiser in his hand.

Sylvie pointed into the living room where Mary was fast asleep in Sam's Lazy Boy, her feet up, eyes closed, the dogs lying on floor beside her.

"Oye, no one's touched my angel food cake," Terri declared, emerging from the kitchen and waving a wooden spoon in the air like a baton.

"That's because we're stuffed," Emma laughed. "You did an amazing job pulling all this together, especially after spending a night in the hoosegow."

"Oh, it wasn't that bad. The bench was softer than my cot in the army," Terri grinned, "and it's been years since I had someone bring me breakfast in bed."

The crowd gathered in the Montana's dining room and kitchen roared with laughter.

Dee's parents had taken their leave after lunch, loaded their horses into their horse trailer, and headed for home. Zoe had already wished the young couple many years of happiness and toddled off to her room with a glass of champagne and a plate of fruit and brownies. Jenny was talking Gus and Cole's ear off on the front porch.

"I think I better go rescue the boys," Sam drawled.

"I'll go with you grandpa," BJ said, joining Sam.

"Scardy-cats," Sylvie joked.

"I'll try a piece of that angel food cake, Terri," Sam heard Dee declare before he exited the house. Where she found room was anyone's guess, Sam grinned.

"Jenny, I'd like you and BJ to go check on Dee's mustang," Sam told his grandkids. "And make sure the other horses have fresh water too. It was a mighty hot day today."

"Yes, sir," BJ nodded, dragging a grumbling Jenny by the arm.

"Since we're alone, Sam," Cole said, glancing through the open door to make sure none of the ladies were nearby. "I was just telling Gus what I found out this morning."

"And that is," Sam inquired, lifting the Budweiser to his lips.

"It appears Cade has a brother," Gus broke in. "He was released last year after doing twenty-five years of hard time. He was in the same penitentiary as Tommy Cortez."

"Cade never mentioned a brother," Sam replied thoughtfully. "And he was incarcerated just down the road you say. Huh!"

"Sylvie's never mentioned a brother-in-law?" Cole asked quietly.

"Not a thing," Sam murmured, putting down his beer.

"Get this: Wallace O'Hara, aka Wally O'Hara, was in for race fixing, murder and fraud," Gus nodded.

"And he was Cade's twin brother," Cole added. "I'm waiting for his case file, but his picture was in the prison records. He and Cade were twins alright – identical twins."

"Is that so," Sam ventured cautiously, his gut churning.

What was Cole implying, Sam wondered? Did he think Sylvie was covering up for Cade's brother or that she and Cade's brother had orchestrated her husband's murder?

Sam's heart constricted. Heartburn settled in his chest like a red-hot poker. Was he in love with a cold-blooded killer? For the first time since the saucy Sylvie O'Hara had moved into his home, he was questioning his judgement.

No! No, he didn't believe it.
Sylvie hadn't killed anyone.

He had been with Sylvie at the morgue. The corpse looked like Cade, but was it? Had they buried Cade or his brother Wally yesterday?

"Let's leave this until tomorrow, gents," Sam rumbled. "Let's not spoil this special day."

"Agreed," Cole responded.

"Agreed," Gus confirmed as Dee stumbled out the door and into her fiancé's arms, a tell tale look on her face.

"You've got other things to contend with," Cole said to Gus.

***

Sam knocked politely on Sylvie's bedroom door after their guests had gone home and the rest of the household had gone to bed. Mary was the only one downstairs; she was sleeping so peacefully in Sam's chair that Sam had covered his old friend with a blanket and tucked her in. The two dogs snored away on the floor beside the chair, happy to be indoors for the night.

"Come on in, Sam," Sylvie replied sleepily.

"I need to ask you a question," Sam whispered hoarsely, opening and then closing the door behind him. He walked over and sat down on the lip of Sylvie's bed.

"Anything, handsome," she murmured through shuttered eyes.

"Did you know Cade had a brother?"

"Wally?" Sylvie gaped, her eyes popping open. "I completely forgot about him. In all these years, I've never met the man. Come to think of it, I've never even seen a family picture with him in it. He and Cade had a falling out shortly before Cade and I met. Wally wasn't invited to our wedding either. Cade was vehement about it."

"So, you didn't know they were twins," Sam snapped.

"What? No way," Sylvie hissed, sitting up. "I don't believe it! Surely, Cade would have told me if he had a twin."

"Cole told me tonight," Sam softened.

Sylvie simmered. There was no mistaking the flame in her eyes or angry set to her jaw.

"You remember something?" he asked her.

"The trouble Cade got into," Sylvie nodded thoughtfully. "He was accused of fraud, fixing bets, that sort of thing. The case was dismissed. I remember something about a mistaken identity, but it was so long ago I can't be sure. I wasn't there. I was in Canada riding in the National Cup at the time. Cade was still angry when he arrived in Calgary and refused to talk about it. I decided to let well enough alone. Maybe I shouldn't have."

"Maybe not," Sam agreed. "Anyway, Cole wants to talk to you about it tomorrow. If he calls and I'm not here for some reason, I wanted you to know what it was about."

"And you wanted to ask me about Wally first," Sylvie smirked.

Sam was silent. He leaned over and kissed Sylvie on the cheek. She smelled of suntan lotion, lime and tequila. Sylvie turned her head, wrapped her arms around his neck and kissed him passionately.

Sam lost himself to the kiss, to the pent-up desire, and sheer wonder of it.

"You better go now, cowboy," she whispered huskily, "I need my beauty sleep."

"Yes, ma'am," he croaked, wanting more than anything to not let her go.

***

"Get up," Sylvie demanded, shaking Maggie awake.

"Wassup," Maggie stammered, fumbling for a light.

"Don't turn on the light," Sylvie hissed, slapping Maggie's hand away from the light switch by the bed. "Get dressed and get your wallet."

"Why," Maggie grumbled.

"Because we're going to Del Mar," Sylvie quipped. "We're going to the track to ask some questions. The Del Mar Debutant and Futility are coming up. If they were there for the Derby, the horses and jockeys should be there for those races as well."

"Oh, I see," Maggie replied, tossing aside her sheets, her voice rising.

"Shhhhh," Sylvie warned her friend.

"You think the woman he's been cheating on us with might be there, don't you?" Maggie said, emboldened. "Right, I'm on it."

Sylvie shook her head in consternation. She watched silently as Maggie got dressed, the light filtering through the crack in the bedroom door enough to illuminate the bedroom. Emma always left a night light on in the bathroom. Maggie threw some extra clothes into an overnight bag, grabbed her purse, double checked her overnight bag, threw another makeup kit into it, and then was ready to go.

The two women tiptoed out of Maggie's room. Zoe opened her door and stumbled into the hall, heading for the bathroom.

"Where are you two going in the middle of the night," she croaked.

"Shhhhhh," Sylvie and Maggie warned their friend.

"We're going to Del Mar to catch a killer," Sylvie replied.

"And the witch that slept with our Cade," Maggie hissed.

"Hold on, let me pee and I'll pack a bag, I'm coming with," Zoe whispered delightedly.

"No," Sylvie spat, but it was too late, Zoe was in the bathroom.

"We'll be downstairs," Maggie said to the closed bathroom door.

Sylvie and Maggie crept down the stairs.

"Where are you two going," Mary croaked sleepily. "And why do you have a packed bag in your hands, Maggie? And why is your suitcase by the door, Sylvie?"

"Quiet," Sylvie shushed her. This was not going as planned. "Don't wake Sam."

"Oh, okay," Mary nodded, throwing the blanket off her. The two dogs woke up, looked over at Maggie and Sylvie, and then lowered their heads once again.

"You haven't answered my question. Why do you both have bags," Mary asked, rubbing the sleep from her eyes.

"We're going sleuthing," Sylvie replied.

"I'm Sherlock and this is Watson," Maggie giggled, nodding towards Sylvie. "We're on the trail of a cheating sod's killer."

"Then I'll be Agatha Christie," Mary beamed, heading for the stairs. "I'll meet you outside."

Heavens, what had she started, Sylvie cringed?

"We better leave a note for Emma and Sam," Maggie said, looking towards the small table where a pad of paper and a pen sat beside the phone charger. "Sam will have the FBI hunting us down if we don't."

"You're right," Sylvie stammered, stopping at the table beside the door, "but what should I say. You know what Sam will do if I tell him where we've gone and why."

"Tell him we decided to hide out in Vegas for a few days until the press has gone," Maggie grinned. "He'll believe that; we've done it before."

"True," Sylvie smiled back and scribbled out a note.

"Speaking of which," Maggie added. "You need a hat. We don't want the press recognizing you at the airport."

"Good idea," Sylvie said, grabbing one of the pink cowboy hats lined up on pegs by the door. Cade had bought the hats for the ladies as a joke. They wore them on poker nights. Sylvie felt a stabbing pain in her chest. Lord, she missed the man and regretted killing him every day.

Wait! She hadn't killed him, right?

Mary and Zoe skipped down the stairs, each of them carrying travel bags. Their eyes shone with delight.

"Ooh, what a great idea, the cowgirl grandmas ride again," Zoe cooed, snatching her cowboy hat off a peg.

"We've decided that Zoe will be Agatha and I'll be Jessica Fletcher," Mary sang happily, plopping her cowboy hat on her head.

"Shhhh," Sylvie and Maggie hissed together.

With a shrug, Maggie grabbed the last hat and put it on. "When in Rome."

Mary and Zoe giggled as Sylvie quietly opened the door and the four women slipped into the night, the cowgirl posse on the trail of a killer, their pink cowboy hats marking their progress in the dawn's early light.

Chapter Fifteen

Life is like a wild horse, you ride it, or it rides you.

"Did any of you notice that black sedan parked on the side of the road alongside the highway outside the ranch?" Mary asked softly from the back seat of Sylvie's large dually pickup truck.

"You don't have to whisper anymore, Mary," we're in Sylvie's truck," Maggie chuckled from the front passenger seat.

"Oh, right. Well, did you?"

"I didn't but there's a Mardi Gras going on in my head," Zoe hissed. "Anyone have a Tylenol?"

Maggie and Mary rummaged through their purses.

"I saw it," Sylvie nodded. "There were two goons asleep in the front seat. Even my headlights didn't wake them up."

"Who do you think they were?" Maggie queried, handing a bottle of Tylenol over the arm rest.

"Thanks," Zoe mumbled, reaching for the bottle.

"No idea and don't care," Sylvie quipped. "Give me one of those Tylenol's when you're done. There are a couple bottles of water in the pockets behind the seat."

"Darned bubbly," Zoe moaned, fumbling around for a water bottle. She downed a couple of painkillers and then handed the open water bottle and two pills to Sylvie.

"How do you think we should handle this?" Mary inquired. "Do we stay together or split up when we get there."

"I think Maggie and I should pair up," Maggie offered. "We make a pretty good team."

"The Soldaderas de la Madre Maria ride again," Zoe shouted, raising a fist into the air. "Ouch, that hurt."

"Viva la soldaderas," Mary agreed, fist bumping Zoe.

Sylvie chuckled. She glanced sideways at Maggie. Maggie smiled thinly, her dark eyes glittering in the light cast by the dash. It was good to see her friend content. Maybe they needed to sneak out of the house at the crack of dawn more often.

"I agree with Maggie. We should stay in couples," Sylvie said, coasting along the highway towards the airport. "You and Zoe head to the stables when we get to the track, Mags. I bet there are a lot of stable workers who will recognize you guys instantly. They'll open up to the soldaderas. Mary and I will see if we can find anyone who remembers Cade among the bookies and ticket sellers. The Del Mar racetrack grounds are huge. It's a long way between the stables, warm up track, and the main concourse."

"And let's not forget the bimbos," Mary chirped. "We need to discover who Cade was involved with and get your money back, Sylvie."

"'Bimbos' is putting it nicely," Maggie murmured, her good mood disappearing.

Sylvie sighed as the airport sign flashed by. She hoped Sam wouldn't be too angry with them. Sam would know they hadn't gone to Vegas. She never gave a thought to Emma.

***

Sam was startled awake. He didn't know what woke him, but he hustled out of bed and into his boots, his instincts telling him something was wrong.

Dawn was breaking in a magnificent display of pinks and reds outside his bedroom window. He strode out of his bedroom and into the living room expecting trouble. Sylvie's bedroom door was closed. The light from the upstairs bathroom illuminated the upper hall and the stairwell. Something wasn't right, he could feel it.

He crept through the house, the hairs on the back of his neck standing on end. A wet tongue brushed his fingers. Sam started and looked down to see Bulldozer's soulful eyes staring up at him. Her son was behind her, tail wagging.

That was when it donned on him. Mary was gone, the lap blanket he had placed over her was on the floor by the Lazy Boy.

"Why aren't you two upstairs with Mary," Sam asked the dogs. He scratched Bulldozer behind the ears, the feeling of 'wrongness' still with him.

The two giant dogs walked over to the door. They looked from the door to him and back again.

"Okay, okay, I got it," Sam chuckled, opening the door.

Sylvie's note floated to the floor.

Sam picked it up as the dogs rushed outside. He turned on the porch light and stepped outside to read it.

"Vegas, my ass," he growled, reading the note.

The dogs' attention was fixed on a vehicle in the distance. Sam saw the glint of the sunrise off the windshield. The car was parked beside the ditch along the highway.

"Damn reporters," he spat.

"What's going on," Emma asked worriedly. "I had a bad feeling and got up to check on the ladies. Maggie, Zoe and Mary are gone."

"Sylvie too," Sam fumed, handing Emma the note.

"Vegas? I don't think so," Emma snapped. "I bet they took off to try and track down Cade's killer."

"They're crazy enough to do it," Sam's baritone rumbled.

"Who's that out there," Emma said, nodding towards the car in the distance.

"That's what I'm going to go find out," Sam declared, brushing by her to go retrieve his shotgun.

"Sam, you be careful. Let me call Cole," Emma pleaded.

Sam silently stalked by her, shotgun already in hand. "You stay back with Emma," he ordered the dogs.

Sam strode down the lane, shotgun propped under one arm as the sun crested the valley to the east, his boots crunching on gravel.

He cautiously approached the ebony Chrysler sedan. Two men were inside, one snoring heavily, his head rolled back over the headrest, and the other man was slumped against the window. Their jackets were open, the butts of their handguns clearly visible in their shoulder harnesses.

Sam tapped the shotgun barrel against the window.

Both men shot forward, reaching for their handguns as they did so.

"I wouldn't," Sam declared, pointing the shotgun in their faces. "Who are you and what do you want?"

The men raised their hands.

The big one behind the driver's seat mimed opening the window. Sam nodded and clicked back the triggers on both barrels. The driver got the point.

"We aren't here for you," the driver rumbled through the now open window.

"Do I need to repeat myself," Sam asked, tapping the shotgun barrel on the windowsill.

"Look, we just want to ask the lady a few questions," the pudding faced goon in the passenger seat replied.

"Her husband has some debts, you know what I mean," the driver grimaced. "The debt has to be paid."

"It does, does it?" Sam growled.

"Yeah, he owes our boss eight big ones," pudding face said.

"That's too bad," Sam snorted. "Not my problem unless you make it one."

The two men nodded in understanding. They weren't dumb. The silver haired cowboy with the silver moustache had that hard frontier vibe about him that they'd only seen in movies up until now.

"The lady needs to pay it, you know, from the winnings, and then we can leave, let bygones be bygones," the big man croaked, the hands on the steering wheel twitching.

"Move those fingers again and you won't live long enough to tell your boss the money is gone," Sam seethed. "Whoever killed Cade O'Hara took the money. That is your boss's problem, not Sylvie's, not now, not ever, you got that. If I see either of you two around here again, you're going to disappear into those mountains up there. There's an old mine with a really deep shaft. I know there are a few skeletons in it. It ain't safe to bring 'em up."

"Yes, sir," pudding face squeaked.

Sam stepped back.

The big man went to roll up the window, and Sam thundered: "Don't ever mess with my family again!"

The mob debt collectors put the car in gear and reversed slowly along the shoulder. Sam looked down the barrel of his shotgun, feet apart, eyes fixed on the driver. He was the most dangerous one of the two.

The driver flipped him the bird before turning the car around and driving off.

Sam knew they'd be back. If those men touched Sylvie or any of his family, he vowed to make good with his threat.

***

Emma bit her lip as she texted Dee: *Don't tell Gus. Sylvie and the ladies are gone. They left a note saying they went to Vegas, but I checked Sylvie's laptop. It was open to a list of flights to Los Angeles. There's another tab opened on the Del Mar Racetrack page. There R 2 big races this weekend.*

Emma was surprised when Dee sent her an instance response: *Let's go. Ladies can't have all the fun. I'll tell Terri.*

Emma tapped out a reply: *The pastor's a bad influence on you.*

Oh, come on. Remember high school? Release the rebel, girl.

Emma giggled.

You think? Emma messaged.

YES!!!! Saddle up. Let's go bet on some ponies.

What about Gus? Emma responded.

He's too tired to come. Dee messaged, ending the text with a series of wicked devil emojes.

Emma looked up in time to see the car on the highway's headlights pop on. The car performed a U turn and drove away. Sam stood on the highway watching it go. Her father-in-law was going to be furious with her. She didn't even want to think about Cole's response to this craziness.

Emma texted Dee back, biting her lip hard enough to draw blood: *I'm in.*

Chapter Sixteen

La Soldaderas de la Madre Maria ride again

The ladies arrived at Del Mar the day before the big race. They had to book a hotel outside of the grounds because everything was full for race day.

The women decided to maintain their cowgirl image, looking very much the part in pink cowboy hats, riding boots, jeans and diamante studded denim shirts. Zoe had purchased them each a matching silver necklace with a turquoise stone embedded at the top of the horseshoe pendant at the hotel. Mary wore her NBHA Open Barrel Racing belt buckle that she won at the ripe old age of seventy-three, the oldest competitor to date. It was her stallion's last race, a wonderful end to a thrilling career. The other ladies had settled on tooled leather belts with simple silver buckles.

"Mary and I are going to go chat with the men watching the warm-up rides on the small oval," Sylvie said as the cab drove away. "I bet they are either bookies or odds makers for the bookies."

"And we'll head to the stables," Maggie purred.

"What if we're asked for badges or something," Zoe worried.

"Just act like haughty owners," Mary suggested. "You gals know how to do that."

"We do," Maggie grinned, slipping her arm under Zoe's. "Don't we darling?"

Zoe puckered her lips and lifted her chin high into the air.

"Haughty, not cheap hooker," Mary reaffirmed.

Maggie and Zoe waved their fingers at the two and strutted off towards the stables, arm in arm, fanny's wiggling.

"Oh, dear, I shouldn't have said anything," Mary worried.

"They'll do fine," Sylvie laughed.

The two friends ambled towards the open gate. It was a long walk to the warmup track. They should have asked the taxi to take them around to the back entrance. Sylvie pulled out the program she had nabbed at the hotel. The hotel catered to racing fans.

"So, Watson, how do WE play this," Mary whispered as they approached the group of men leaning over the rails scribbling notes on a program as a bay colt cantered by.

"Like prospective owners," Sylvie replied softly. "There's a couple of claiming races later today. We'll chat about those and then switch to Futility prospects and gossip."

"That's a wonderful idea," Mary cooed. "I wonder if that colt that just went by is for sale. It would be fun if we all joined in and bought a racehorse."

"Down girl, we're here to catch a killer, not go broke," Sylvie chuckled.

"Lovely day, gentlemen," Mary said with a wink at Sylvie.

The four men turned, their eyes widening at the two cowgirl grandmas standing in front of them. One man, a carrot topped redhead with warm grey eyes recognized the belt buckle. "You're Mary Adams," he gasped, a wide grin breaking out on his earnest face.

"Who is Mary Adams?" the brunette standing beside him asked briskly, taking in the petite woman wearing a flashy pink cowboy hat. Mary stood no higher than the top of his chest.

"Guys, this lady won the NBHR finals seven or eight years ago," redhead gushed. "You set the world record. No one has beaten it yet."

"I remember you too, Ms Adams," a tall white-haired gent in jeans and open topped white and blue plaid shirt replied. "I won a bundle on you. Odds in Vegas were 150 to 1. Folks thought it was a joke until you and your horse left the rest of the wannabes in the dust in the opening round. By the finals, odds were down to 2 to 1. I bet on you early. That stallion of yours was a powerhouse"

"Well, thank you," Mary blushed. "Patch paid off the rest of my mortgage that day."

"You still have that stud?" silver hair inquired. "I know some folks who'd love to breed to him."

"Patch is retired now," Mary smiled, sidling closer to the handsome senior, "but to the right horse and for the right price, I'd consider it. He's not cheap, I warn you. Four of his offspring are competing and, in the money, and another is the Australian reining champion."

"Tell me more," Mary's new suitor replied, looping Mary's hand under his arm and walking her away from the other men.

Sylvie couldn't help it; she burst out laughing, the other men joining in. Mary wasn't one to brag. Sylvie had no idea Mary was that famous.

"So, what are you here for, little lady," the lanky blond asked. He reminded Sylvie of Tom Brady.

"I've always loved the races," Sylvie lied smoothly. "My late husband was a fan. I was thinking of buying a colt in the claims race this afternoon."

"I wouldn't waste my money on those nags," the brunette said, opening his program.

"Well, I did quite like that bay that cantered by," Sylvie replied smoothly.

"That was Marvelous Marvin," the blond laughed. "He's not in the races today. He's running the Futurity tomorrow. Most of the horses out here right now are in the Futurity. The jockeys are stretching their legs and getting them used to the track.

"That's I Beg Your Pardon coming towards us," the brunette nodded at the chestnut loping by.

"And the grey around the far side of the track is London Fog," offered the redhead. "I'm giving him three to one odds."

"I'd say five to one is the safe bet," Tom Brady argued.

"Nah, I'm listing London Fog as the favourite at two to one," brunette contended.

"Are you all odds makers?" Sylvie smiled, trying to keep it light. "You seem to be very knowledgeable."

The men puffed out their chests. Sylvie's smile got wider. It was nice to know she could still manipulate the opposite sex, even at her age.

"I was thinking of trying to buy that filly, the one that won the derby, One Flashy Dame," Sylvie continued, turning on the charm. "What are your expert opinions on her?"

"Don't waste your money," Tom Brady scoffed.

"The reason she won was the track was a mess and the filly's a mudder," the brunette agreed. "The old lady...er, pardon me... the woman that owned her was smart enough to take her home after her win. I hear she won't run the filly again."

"As a matter of fact, the jockey that rode One Flashy Dame is riding London Fog," the redhead said, nodding toward the diminutive rider atop the dappled grey galloping around the corner towards them.

"But I heard she and the jockey aboard Steam Train were under investigation," Sylvie whispered conspiratorially.

"Not her, she's a straight shooter," Tom Brady grumbled.

Sylvie looked up. *What did he mean by that? Did that jockey throw other races, but this was the first time he was called out on it?* The other men acted as if they hadn't heard him.

"That doesn't mean anything," the brunette mumbled. "Interesting enough London Fog is owned by the same trainer as Steam Train. Fog and Steam train are half-brothers."

"The other jockey is riding Marvellous Marvin," the redhead volunteered. "If he's still riding, he's not under investigation. It's got to sting though, losing his ride to the upstart jockey."

"And why would you ask about him if you're interested in buying One Flashy Dame," the brunette asked suspiciously.

"Because I don't like wasting money," Sylvie purred.

The men roared with laughter.

"Then don't buy a racehorse," the redhead advised her.

"I'll take your advice into consideration," she nodded as Mary and the silver fox ambled back along the rail. Mary sported a cat that ate the cream expression.

"Thank you, gentlemen, I think I'm going to take a walk to the stables and see what is for sale," Sylvie remarked casually.

"Tell security Billy said you're okay if anyone asks," Tom Brady waved.

Sylvie nodded thanks as Mary broke away from her amorous suitor.

"You're positively glowing," Sylvie casually remarked.

"So are you," Mary blushed. "You'll never guess what I found out."

"What?"

"The owner of Steam Train fired his jockey after the race and demanded the track and police question him for fixing the race. Apparently, it even led to fisticuffs."

"The jockey wasn't suspended though," Sylvie whispered as they walked along the rail towards the gate leading to the stables.

"Yes, he was cleared," Mary agreed. "There were rumours the jockey may have taken a bribe, but they couldn't prove it because of the filly's outstanding performance. Get this… Steam Train's owner's wife was reputed to be having an affair with one of the regulars here and it was said he was the man who won big thanks to One Flashy Dame."

"You got all that in twenty minutes," Sylvie exclaimed.

"And a date for dinner," Mary shrugged.

"I can't imagine what you'll discover over dinner," Sylvie purred.

Mary grinned, her face alight with mischief.

***

"Hey, amigos, la Soldaderas de la Madre Maria," a squat muscled middle aged groom yelled down the stable aisles.

Maggie's eyes widened in disbelief as several men dropped their pitchforks and horse brushes and ran towards them. One groom raced over leading a fancy black thoroughbred filly. Zoe removed her hat and fluffed up her spiky hair. Maggie thought it a wasted gesture.

"Hola," Zoe beamed.

"Señoras, it is so nice to meet you," the stable worker grinned. "You are here for the races?"

"Si, we are thinking of buying a horse," Maggie said, taken by the black filly the younger groom was holding, "and thought we'd come take a look at what is available."

"Then you are speaking to the right people," the man whispered to her. He turned to the other grooms and translated Maggie's words into Spanish. The men smiled and nodded like bubble headed dolls.

The filly regarded Maggie with kind intelligent eyes. The horse snorted and gently snuffled the groom's shoulder. While they weren't really supposed to be buying a horse, Maggie liked the filly's disposition and form.

What could it hurt to look at? She was only playing a part, right?

The filly had a broad chest for a two-year-old, thick legs, and strong level quarters. Power rippled through her lines.

"Don't even think about it," Zoe hissed.

Maggie rolled her eyes and pushed through the crowd of men. They parted reverently, a couple reaching out to brush their dirty fingers over her arm. Normally, Maggie would have snapped at them, but she was all eyes on the horse in front of her.

"You don't want this one, señora," the young lad bowed as she approached. "She's not fast."

"Si, we take you to see the best," the first man nodded. "My name is Miguel. I will show you who you should buy if you want to win big."

The other men nodded.

"That one is a mule," another groom said. "She's in the second claiming race tonight. She'll probably go for meat. She's good for nothing."

"Maybe you should listen, Maggie, you already have one mule," Zoe grinned.

"Some are fast, some may even win, but you know," Miguel shrugged, "the fastest don't always do so well."

"What do you mean by that exactly," Zoe asked, catching on to where the groom was heading.

Maggie didn't care. The filly had fixed her with that look, a deep down to the heart moment that only happens when a horse bonds instantly with one singular person, a soul-to-soul connection, one so strong that their fates are forever intertwined.

"What's her name," Maggie asked huskily, reaching out to stroke the filly's soft muzzle. The horse leaned into her hand and sighed.

"A Darker Shade of Black," the lad replied. "I call her Shade. I don't want her to go to meat, but I fear Angelo is right. She is not suited to the track."

"Not on my watch," Maggie growled, straightening up.

"Maggie, no," Zoe hissed.

"You take care of what we're here for," Maggie snorted. "You're a better talker than I am anyway. Shade and I are having a moment."

Zoe shook her head.

"Miguel, tell me everything," Zoe continued. "And thank you all for such a warm greeting. You have made our hearts soar and probably emptied out one of us' wallets."

Maggie chuckled as the men tripped over each other to show Zoe around the stable, chattering away, and revealing many a secret.

"Is there anywhere I can see Shade move out," Maggie asked the groom. "I don't want to see her race; I just want to see her move."

"Si, señora, I can get a lunge line," the lad nodded.

The filly tilted her head towards Maggie and pushed against her shoulder lightly. Maggie laughed.

"The filly, she is the same color as your hair," the lad blushed. "You will look good on top of her, better than on the mule."

"She does have hair the same color as mine, doesn't she?" Maggie agreed. "I guess you saw us on TV. I don't ride the mule anymore. He's happy though."

Maggie already knew her mind was made up. She wasn't going to all Shade to go into any claiming race to end up with some hack or worse, on a trailer heading to the slaughterhouse. Storm had a few breeding years left. If not Storm, then she'd talk to Maggie about breeding the filly to Buddy. What a spectacular jumper this filly could produce.

The more she thought about it, the more she thought breeding the filly to Buddy would be ideal. She'd have to wait a couple of years though. Maggie didn't like breeding a mare before the age of five.

"Oh, sod it, don't worry about lunging her. Get hold of the owner for me, I want to buy her, but don't let on who I am," Maggie ranted. "I don't want him to think I'm a push over."

"The owner isn't a man, she's a lady," the groom replied. "That is her niece there."

Maggie turned to see a young girl riding a spectacular grey colt with dark black dapples on his shoulders and rump walking towards her. The colt's nostrils were flared. His neck and flanks were soaked with sweat.

"Sadie," the lad called to the jockey. "This lady is interested in your aunt's filly."

"Really," the girl grinned. "Isn't she a beauty? Let me get this guy unsaddled and I'll be back."

"Lovely" Maggie beamed, pleased to see the girl jockey. "Take your time. I'm not going anywhere for awhile."

"Miss Sadie won the derby on One Flashy Dame," the lad whispered in Maggie's ear. "Her aunt is mucho loco."

"That's okay, I'm mucho loco too," Maggie replied good-naturedly.

Maggie stood inside Shade's stall rubbing a wet rag down the filly's shiny coat when Sadie Nesbitt arrived, freshly washed and sporting a wide grin, the groom having had to move on to look after the other horses he oversaw.

"It's much too hot here for a black mare," Maggie said, gently stroking the filly while it picked at the flake of hay in the hay net. "You'll love the ranch. There's lots of open spaces and even when it is hot, a breeze blows in from the mountains."

"You've really fallen in love her, haven't you," Sadie grinned. "I can see it in your eyes."

"She is lovely," Maggie replied carefully. She didn't want this girl jockey to think she was a push over. Maggie hadn't felt this way about a horse since she first met her stallion. He was a knot head, but she loved him.

"I can see it in her eyes too," Sadie said. "She's bonded to you already."

Maggie let the remark go unanswered.

"You aren't a cowgirl, are you," Sadie laughed.

"What makes you say that?" Maggie stiffened.

"You're too classy, just like my girl here," Sadie added, stepping into the stall with Maggie. The filly licked her lips and then snuffled the tiny jockey.

"I think Shade would make a wonderful jumper, maybe even a hunter depending on how she matures," Maggie said, realizing it was time to play her hand.

"I agree. Shade is half-sister to One Flashy Dame."

"The long shot that won the derby," Maggie gasped.

"The same," the jockey replied proudly. "Every horse has its day. Flash had hers. Shade is fast, but she doesn't have the heart for racing. I was furious with my aunt for entering her into the claiming race. I'd already set aside the money to buy her myself if I didn't like the outcome."

"Is that so?"

"Yes."

"I'm glad to hear that," Maggie smiled, taking in the diminutive jockey's measure. Maggie liked what she saw. The girl cared about the horses she rode.

"I called my aunt. We've scratched Shade from the race."

Maggie's spirits lifted. Cade's murder and the funeral had knocked her for a loop. For the first time in years, she felt energized.

"How much does your aunt want for her," she asked cautiously.

"Whatever the Soldaderas de la Madre Maria can afford," Sadie grinned. "Don't be surprised. It's all over the track. Gossip travels fast."

Maggie smothered a laugh, her eyes watering with the effort. The race through Mexico and the run across the border on a mule named Cade had changed her – for the better it seemed. Maybe Cade's death was a good thing. She would start anew. Nobody was too old for a fresh start.

"Do you have time for a drink or glass of lemonade," Maggie asked the jockey. "We can settle our account and perhaps you can help me make arrangements to transport our girl here to her new home at the ranch. After that, I'd love to hear more about your epic race."

"I've got two more horses to ride and then I'm all yours for an hour," Sadie clapped happily.

The filly snorted agreement.

***

One town over from the Montana Ranch, Nan's Wildflower Nursery was awaiting a truck load of manure. Nan's Border collie, Frank, saw the truck coming long before Nan. At the same time, two groups of local landscapers arrived, orders in hand. Nan was working at half staff, the summer flu, also known as one of the last days of summer before school starts, had left her working double and triple duty.

The lumbering dump truck rolled into the yard. Frank raced into the parking lot barking furiously.

"Just drop it in the usual spot," Nan yelled at the driver, pointing to the spot where she always kept the organic mulches. "Frank, heel."

The Border collie obeyed her instantly, matching her pace through the greenhouses as she rolled the cart, filling the landscapers' orders for fall flowers.

The driver honked and waved after he unloaded the five yards of all-natural fertilizer. Nan didn't notice him; she was too busy, but Frank did.

Frank whined, his head lowered, tail between his hind legs, waiting for the order to go.

"Okay, okay, off you go," Nan chuckled.

The dog shot off like a bullet.

Chapter Seventeen

The love for a horse is just as complicated as the love for another human being...If you never love a horse, you will never understand.

The ladies sat in the hotel room a bottle of open California merlot on the table in front of them. They had already made their way through two cheese and fruit platters and were munching away on a tray of desserts.

"That was an eventful day," Mary cried happily, picking up a lemon meringue tart.

"I'll say," Sylvie sighed wearily.

"We think we know who Cade was involved with," Mary said through a mouthful of tart.

"Hmmm, some bleached blond sagging bimbo if the rumors are true," Zoe snapped, swishing the wine in her glass in circles.

"Does it really matter," Maggie grunted. "Maybe we should let it rest, Sylvie."

Sylvie eyed her friend dubiously.

"We can't do that," Zoe gasped. "Not now!"

"And not since we're already here," Mary agreed.

"You just want to go home and play with your new filly," Zoe grumbled.

"What new filly?" Mary and Sylvie asked in unison.

"A Shade Darker Than Black," Zoe grinned.

"You'll love her when you see her," Maggie answered calmly.

Good gosh, another horse? What was Maggie thinking? She was in her seventies? It was time to slow done, not start breeding horses again.

"She is very fancy," Zoe added, sipping her wine, and then to Maggie, her face a picture of innocence. "And she's the same color as Maggie's hair, if that is your real hair color."

Maggie smirked.

"You weren't supposed to actually buy a horse, only look at them," Mary boomed.

"Zoe looked at them," Maggie grinned cheekily over top of her wine glass. "Besides, I found out something better."

"What's that?" Sylvie asked pointedly.

"The woman that owned Shade owned One Flashy Dame," Maggie purred. "I had tea with the jockey, who it so happens is the owner's niece. She was the one who gave Cade the tip that Flash loved running in the mud. She easily picked out the picture of Cade I showed her on my phone."

"Wow," Mary exploded.

"The race wasn't fixed, it was a fluke," Maggie added. "Cade was well known around the track. He won big and lost big, numerous times. I can also confirm who the bleached blond bimbo was."

Sylvie held her breath.

"Oooh, I know, I know," Mary cried, waving her hand in the air like a schoolgirl.

"Lacy Finnigan," Maggie said solemnly.

"She is Sean Finnigan's wife, Steam Train's owner," Mary agreed. "Bart told me over dinner."

"And Finnigan has a horse in the Futurity tomorrow," Zoe added. "The grooms showed him to me. He's a nasty piece of work, but from what Miguel told me, so is the owner. He's not kind to his horses."

"A grey, London Fog," Sylvie nodded. "That girl Sadie was riding him. She flew by us. Apparently, he is half-brother to Steam Train."

"Oh, I saw him too," Maggie piped up. "He didn't look nasty, but Sadie has a way with horses. They adore her. Maybe the colt doesn't like men."

"Probably that owner's doing. Can you blame the man though if his wife was running around with Cade," Sylvie admitted? Betrayal of that sort did more than break the heart. Still, she'd never take out her anger on a horse.

"There's more," Zoe added, finishing her wine. "Scuttle butt was that Cade owed money to more than one bookie... and a couple of jockeys. Those odds calculator dudes you met today think the grooms and stable cleaners don't speak English, but they do. One of the cleaners told me that one of the guy's bosses was still owed a lot of money."

"I wonder if those two guys sleeping in their car at the ranch were looking for me," Sylvie blanched, the cream puff she just ate threatening to come up.

"Maybe we should head home," Maggie suggested, her brows knitting together in worry.

"You just want to play with your new pony," Zoe quipped, tossing back a lemon tart.

"No, we'll stay together," Sylvie replied stubbornly. No bookie was going to run her off. "I want to know who killed Cade."

"Follow the money," Mary nodded sagely. "That's what Agatha would do."

"Sherlock, Watson, and Jessica too," Zoe agreed, wiping the pastry crumbs from her lips with one finger. "You know I think all the shows on TV say that."

"My money is on one of the bookies who didn't send men to the funeral," Maggie purred. "I bet whoever did it took the money out of the trunk after he killed Cade."

"Yes, but it might have been a crime of passion," Mary said. "I think it was the cheating wife's husband."

"It may also have been a crooked jockey," Sylvie added, looking from one of her friends to the other, "like maybe one that didn't get paid after throwing a big race?"

"You mean the jockey who rode Steam Train," Zoe queried. "The boys at the track hinted that I should never bet on a horse he was riding no matter the odds."

"That is interesting," Mary whispered.

"Even more interesting is he is riding Marvelous Marvin in the Futurity and Marvin is one of the favorites," Sylvie noted smugly.

"There were a few other jockeys riding the day Cade won big too. Two of them are riding tomorrow," Zoe confirmed. "As a matter of fact, Miguel told me to watch for Razzle Dazzle Me. He whispered in my ear that the colt was being held back and if I wanted to buy a winner, I should talk to the owner. Funnily enough, he said if I bought the horse, I should ask Sadie Nesbitt to ride him."

"Well, Maggie already bought one horse," Sylvie chuckled, "but that doesn't mean we can't all look into something with a little more razzle dazzle."

"You think?" Mary laughed.

"I'm in," Zoe grinned. "I've got more money than I know what to do with anyway. I've already decided to give Expresso to BJ."

"Whoops," Sylvie stuttered, glancing sideways at Maggie.

"That's a marvelous idea," Maggie nodded. "You should get a DNA test done though. I was studying that colt the other day. He looks more like a Buddy baby than Storm's, don't you agree, Sylvie?"

"I do," Sylvie croaked.

"It's funny, I was thinking the same thing," Zoe smirked, amused. "I ordered it last week. Hopefully, we'll hear back by mid-month."

"Good to know," Maggie replied sagely. "BJ is a natural choice. He is young and so is the colt. Expresso will have a home for life. What more can any of us ask of our horses?"

"Here, here," Sylvie chimed, refilling everyone's wine glasses.

"And here is to a prosperous day tomorrow," Mary cheered, lifting her glass in the air.

The ladies clinked glasses.

"Now, spill the beans," Sylvie quipped, leaning forward. "Tell us all about your dinner with the Bartman."

Mary turned a deep shade of candy apple red. The ladies then toasted her future romance.

***

Sam, BJ, and Jenny sauntered into the house, itchy, tired, sweaty, and stomachs growling. They had just finished unloading and stacking two hundred fifty-pound square bales of hay into the barn's loft. It was the last of the summer cut. The rest was packaged in round bales in an outside storage shed. The cows got the round bales; the horses got the better grade orchard grass from the barn.

It was so late when they were done that it was time to feed the horses, so they did that as well before coming in.

"I'm starved," Jenny whined.

"Me too, baby girl," Sam chortled.

"Mom, what's for dinner," BJ hollered.

BJ's call was met with silence.

"You two go clean up and I'll check on supper," Sam grunted.

The kids raced up the stairs, vying for who got to shower first.

Sam strolled into the kitchen. He could smell the roast beef warming in the oven. There was a note on the table.

"Not another damnable note," he mumbled.

'Gone to LA with the girls – Dee and Terri that is. Back Monday. Roast, potatoes, carrots and gravy warming in the oven. Fresh muffins in the fridge. Love Emma.'

"You have got to be kidding me," Sam growled, heading back into the living room to look for the phone. He dialed Gus' cell number.

"Hello," Gus answered.

Sam could hear the din of people talking excitedly in the background.

"It's Sam. Where are you?"

"On the East coast working the case," Gus answered. "I left early this morning. Why? What's wrong?"

"Have you talked to Dee or your sister lately?"

"What kind of trouble have they gotten into now," Gus rumbled. "I never knew Dee had such a wild streak. My sister is a given."

"Be glad you never met Dee in high school," Sam chuckled briefly. "She was a hellion. So was Emma. I thought they'd grown out of it. Seems the girls have taken off to LA. I can guess what they're doing there."

"Oh, no," Gus shouted into the phone as the noise behind him got louder. "This is serious, Sam. We're preparing to take down Harry the Hammer. Those two goons at the funeral were his. Our sources say they just arrived back in town."

"Yeah, I ran them off at dawn this morning," Sam replied worriedly. "They must have been on the plane after yours. You think they can track Sylvie and the gals to LA?"

"I don't know," Gus yelled. "I'll call Cole and get him on it. I'm stuck here for now."

"Alright, I'll wait to hear from one or the other of you," Sam hollered back, hanging up.

Sam's hands shook. Gus, the two goons, and Sylvie and the ladies were all at the airport at the same time. It was only dumb luck that they didn't spot Sylvie and the ladies.

"Where's mum," BJ asked, entering the kitchen, his raven hair still wet from the shower.

"She's gone on a mini-vacation with Dee and Terri. She'll be back in a couple of days. Mean time, I think we can look after ourselves. Mum left a roast in the oven."

"Sure," BJ shrugged. "I can help."

Sam marveled at his grandson. He took everything in stride. Jenny was another matter. There would be some righteous howling going on tonight without her mother to tuck her in.

Sam sighed. He prayed the women weren't in over their heads... all of them!

***

Nan was the last to leave the nursery. She double checked the heat lamps in the building housing the indoor plants and made sure the water hoses were all off outside. She hadn't seen Frank in some time, but the day had gotten busier and busier. Now, the sun was almost set, and stars twinkled behind the half moon hanging just above the horizon.

"Frank, here boy," she called as she locked up the main greenhouse and office space.

Nan heard a guttural growl in the dark and then saw Frank dragging something towards her across the empty parking lot beneath the security lights.

"What have you got there boy," she asked the dog.

With the money wallet with the days till's contents under her arm, she walked over to her dog. She stopped short when she saw what lay in the drive.

"Where's the lower half, Frank? You didn't eat it, did you?"

***

Cole hung up the phone in his office, his face mottled with anger. He couldn't believe Emma had run off with Dee and Terri to LA to help those crazy old broads try to solve Cade O'Hara's murder. What were those women thinking? Gus was as furious as he was.

Gus and his team were about to bust Harry the Hammer for drug trafficking, arms dealing, and illegal gambling…these crooks and their monikers…thought they were all Al Capone's. It meant Gus was tied up on the East coast though so that left him champing at the bit.

Maybe he should catch a flight to LA in the morning? One of his deputies could fill in for a couple of days. Cole didn't know what he'd do if anything happened to Emma.

He was about to leave for the night, when the night clerk called him over.

"What is it," Cole snapped, irritated.

"Sorry, Cole, it's Nan over at the nursery. Seems Frank dug up a body. Nan's not sure if'n he ate half of it or not. Says she'll let us know in the morning after he has his constitutional, only she didn't put it quite that way."

"Not another one," Cole muttered. "Call everyone in. Have them meet me at the nursery. Oh, and call the coroner's office too."

"Already did," the night clerk replied.

Cole put on his hat and headed out the door, his shoulders slumping in defeat.

***

Cole stood in the morgue looking down on yet another body. His face was lined with exhaustion. It was all he could do to keep from falling over. He looked at the clock on the wall: it was two in the morning.

The remains on the metal gurney looked eerily familiar. There wasn't much flesh left, but the strands of long silver hair attached to the back of the skull, coupled with the fact that the shreds of material hanging off the bones looked suspiciously like flannel pajamas, made him wonder if the corpse on the gurney was the real Cade O'Hara?

Sylvie had confessed to smothering her husband. Sam swore he had seen Cade's corpse in the outhouse. Maggie and Sylvie had also insisted Cade was dead, especially after they pushed his body out Maggie's second story bedroom window.

Cole examined the corpse's lower half. The crime scene techs had found it, still buried in the manure compost mix.

"It's pretty degraded, but manure will do that to a corpse," the coroner said, bending over the body. "The microbes devour the flesh in under thirty days, especially if the manure is turned and aerated regularly. The teeth and hair are intact though so we should be able to get some pretty good DNA. By the looks of the hyoid bone, I think this man was strangled, possibly suffocated. I'll let you know when I've completed the full autopsy."

"I see," Cole grimaced, feeling the blood drain from his face. "Question for you, Doc: can identical twins have the same DNA?"

"Oh, yes. It is rare, but it happens. Identical twins may look the same at first, but after a while small differences emerge such as one being taller than the other, or their eyes or hair are a slightly different shade. There are documented cases though of twins who have the exact same fingers prints and DNA molecules. It is a fascinating field of study. Why do you ask?"

"I've seen the body's hair before… on the victim you looked at a couple weeks ago," Cole replied. "Cade O'Hara. Do you remember him? I discovered he had a twin."

"I do remember him. We don't get a lot of murder victims through here, hunting accidents and the like, but not executions. And you think this might be the twin?" the coroner queried. "Wouldn't that be a lark, eh?"

"Not really," Cole mumbled.

If this was Cade, who three women admittedly strangled, then who had they buried last Saturday? Wally?

Was Wally using Cade's name to deflect suspicion off his illegal activities not realizing his brother was dead? Or, was this Wally, and Cade was the one who was shot out on the highway?

"I'll do a quick DNA swab and send it off to the lab requesting a comparison to the DNA they are already working on," the coroner said. "I'll call the lab myself this afternoon and tell them it is coming."

"Thanks, Doc," Cole said, heading for the door.

Cole left the morgue quickly, his mind on overload. If that was Cade in there, then he would have to arrest Sylvie O'Hara for murder, and possibly even Maggie Carroll and Zoe Puddicombe as accessories to murder. Would the killer still target Sylvie or the Montana family believing it all to be too coincidental?

Gus was already involved in the first case. Cole had no problem bringing in the senior ATF agent on this one. For all they knew, Cade and Wally O'Hara may have been killed for the same reason. Cade may still have walked away from the ranch the day he disappeared. Stranger things had happened.

"Yeah, let's just spread the burden around," Cole sighed, unlocking the door to his suburban. "Maybe after I get a few hours' sleep."

Chapter Eighteen

A polo handicap is a persons ticket to the world. Sir Winston Churchill

Cole sat up straight in bed. He struggled to remember what he was dreaming about, and then it hit him as hard as the linebacker that took out his knee and shoulder, snapping the bones like an oak tree in a category six hurricane.

He leapt out of bed. It was five thirty in the morning. The sun hadn't even come up yet.

Cole picked up his cell phone, about to wake up Gus when a text message came in.

'You up?'

Cole smirked and dialled his friend.

"I'm up," Cole said. "I'm getting dressed and heading to the airport."

"Me too, I'm already in route," Gus said, his voice crackling. "Listen, I found out something about an hour ago."

"I know," Cole cut him off as he slipped on his jeans. "It was Wally O'Hara we just buried, not Cade."

"How'd you figure that out," Gus chuckled. "Have you been holding out on me? I always thought you were Sheriff Howdy Doody not Sam Spade."

"Hardy-har-har. Cade O'Hara is on a slab in my morgue. A Border collie named Frank found his body in a recently delivered batch of manure. The Montana's use the same company for picking up their manure pile," Cole hissed, tugging on his boots. "I don't know how Cade ended up in the manure pile, but he did. How'd you figure it out?"

"Harry told us," Gus said, his voice sounding even more distant.

"You're starting to break up," Cole said, reaching for a shirt.

"Harry told us Wally started using Cade's name as a cover so that he could get back onto the track," Gus shouted. "The mob killed the jockey who double crossed Wally fixing a race years ago. The mob was out hundreds of thousands of dollars. Wally went down for the murder to settle his debt. Guess he wanted to start back up where he left off all those years ago."

"That makes sense," Cole agreed. "Your guy turning on his bosses?"

"Yeah, we cut a deal," Gus yelled, his voice still coming and going. "I have to…. meet you in …"

"Gus…"

The phone went dead.

Cole tugged on his shirt, grabbed his gun, badge, and wallet and headed for the airport. He texted Gus on the way out the door that he'd message him when he arrived in LA. Cole assumed that was what Gus was going to say before they lost the connection.

All Cole knew was his spider senses were tinkling. Emma and the girls were in danger. He thought about calling Sam but decided against it. Sam had enough to worry about, plus he had the kids and all the horses to deal with.

"Bwock, bwock," Cole muttered.

He was being a chicken and he knew it. Cole was going to have to arrest Sylvie. Emma might never speak to him again, little own agree to marry him.

"Sometimes I hate this job," he croaked.

Chapter Nineteen

If anybody expects to calm a horse down by tiring him out with riding swiftly and far, his supposition is the reverse of the truth.
Xenophon

Emma knocked softly on the door to room 638.

"You can't tell me they aren't up yet, it's ten a.m.," Terri snorted.

"Knock harder," Dee suggested when nobody answered.

Emma shrugged and pounded her fist against the door.

"Open up in the name of the Law," Terri bellowed.

A couple of doors squeaked open, angry faces peering out at them.

The three women, a brunette and two redheads, one peach colored, the other flaming red, covered their mouths with their hands to stifle an uncontrollable fit of the giggles.

"Law, schmaw, it's too early to get arrested," Sylvie grumbled, opening the door in bare feet and a long white cotton shirt that fell halfway between her thighs and her knees. Her hair was a tangled mess.

"That's one of Sam's shirts?" Emma blurted out.

"Emma, Dee," Sylvie yelled, her bleary eyes opening wide.

Two doors down, someone slammed their door shut.

"What about me?" Terri cried, feigning indignation.

"You too," Sylvie laughed. "How on earth did you find us?"

"I called every hotel near the track looking for my four crazy pink cowboy hat clad aunties," Emma shrugged, eyes overflowing with mirth. "Okay, I told the clerk you were my mother. He took one look at me and gave me your room number."

"It helped that she was accompanied by a priest," Terri snorted.

"And a forest ranger," Dee added. "I showed him my credentials."

"Come in, come in," Sylvie said with a shake of her head, ushering the girls into the suite.

Empty wine bottles, dirty glasses, and platters of empty food trays littered the room.

"We missed the party," Dee sulked.

"It wasn't exactly a party, more like a powwow," Sylvie snickered, "with options."

"Who's here so early?" Maggie moaned, walking out of her room looking as fresh as ever in her silk nightgown and long silken hair. "Surely, Zoe and Mary aren't up yet?"

Maggie stopped abruptly when she saw the three younger women taking in the condition of the suite, large grins on their faces.

"What are you doing here," Maggie asked, taken by surprise.

"We came to help," Emma smirked, hands on her hips.

"Lovely," Maggie replied. "The more the merrier."

Emma glanced sideways at Sylvie. A warm reception from Maggie? Was it the Apocalypse? Invasion of the body snatchers? Her look must have said it all because Sylvie replied, "Maggie bought a horse."

"Oh, that explains everything," Dee rolled her eyes at Emma.

"Does Sam know?" Emma snorted.

"Not yet," Sylvie rolled her eyes. "Coffee?"

"Oh, yes, please," Terri agreed, heading over to the small kitchenette to brew a fresh pot of coffee.

"Wait until you meet her, Emma," Maggie continued, sweeping towards the telephone. "She's stunning. Have you gals eaten yet? Otherwise, I'll just order Sylvie and I something."

"Who are you and what did you do with our Maggie," Emma whispered.

"I'm starved," Terri interrupted.

"Yeah, what do they have that's good here," Dee beamed. "I could eat a horse, but I'd settle for bacon, two eggs over easy, taters and whole wheat toast."

"Me too," Terri agreed.

"Me three," Emma nodded, her mouth watering. "All we've eaten since last night was three-day old sandwiches from a machine at the airport."

"Make it breakfast for five, Mags, and coffee... a lot more coffee," Sylvie added.

Sylvie cleared the table, piling the empty food trays on top of each other and taking them over to the kitchen. Emma rushed over to help, scooping up all the empty plastic wine glasses and tossing them into the nearest waste bin, while Dee and Terri fixed coffee for everyone.

"Maggie's had an epiphany," Sylvie whispered to Emma.

"It must have been some epiphany," Emma murmured.

"Hmmm, she told me last night she realized yesterday while looking at A Darker Shade of Black, that's her new filly's name, that she didn't want to waste the rest of her life being bitter. She wanted to let it all go. Between Cade's murder, her adventure over the border and subsequent ride through the desert on a mule, she was capable of much more than she ever thought she was."

"That filly must be really something," Emma snorted, not sure what to make of Maggie's newfound niceness.

"She is actually. She seems to have a calming effect on Maggie. Oh, and Maggie is thrilled that Zoe wants to give Expresso to BJ," Sylvie chortled. "She even suggested a DNA test to determine his paternity."

"Still my beating heart," Emma said. "I can't believe one racehorse did all that."

"I'm not sure either," Sylvie grinned. "Time will tell."

There was another knock at the door. Terri and Dee raced to open it, giggling like three-year-old's.

"Dee," Mary shouted, bustling through the door.

"Preacher," Zoe smiled. "Wonderful! We'll have to think up more detective names!"

"You better add two more breakfasts to the order," Maggie told the desk clerk on the other end of the phone.

"Did Maggie tell you about her new horse," Mary gushed.

"And that we're thinking of going in on a racehorse named Marvelous Marvin," Zoe chattered on. "Marvelous, don't you think? He's racing today in the Futurity. His jockey is crooked. My friend Miguel told me."

"Please tell me Marvelous Marvin isn't another stud?" Emma thundered. "Sam will have a fit."

"Oh, don't worry, dear, we've already talked to Sadie," Mary said, waving a hand in the air. "She's our new jockey and trainer. You'll love her. Once Marvin loses today, we should be able to get him for a song. He'll go to Sadie's auntie's stable. Wait until you see that girl ride."

Emma didn't know what to say: sudden epiphanies, a new thoroughbred filly, crooked jockeys, a racehorse syndicate, and detective names? Forget the coffee, she needed something stronger, and it wasn't even noon yet. How on earth were they going to break all this news to her father-in-law? And where were they going to put another horse in the barn?

"Go with the flow," Terri whispered, cupping a hand under her arm for support. "Just breathe deeply and relax."

"Easier said than done," Emma mumbled.

Chapter Twenty

If a horse stands on you, it is because you are in its way

The racetrack was a hive of activity when the ladies arrived in two taxis. The stands were bursting with betters of all ages, races, and sexes. Mary's new beau, Bart, waited at the main gate. He held up four VIP passes as the women approached him.

"And who are these lovely young ladies," he purred, eyeing Dee and Emma with open admiration.

"These are our friends, Emma Montana, Dee soon-to-be Rodriquez, and Pastor Terri Scallon," Mary grinned, whisking the passes out of Bart's hand.

"A pastor no less," the silver tongued handsome senior grinned. "Maybe you can say a few prayers over my betting stubs? Couldn't hurt, could it?"

"I don't think the big guy would approve," Terri laughed, "but, hey, I'll give it a try for you."

"Sorry, I don't have more VIP passes for you girls," Bart said, looking positively contrite.

"That's okay, we're here to have a little fun," Emma smiled, waving a twenty-dollar bill in the air, "and I have twenty to prove it."

"She's a real big spender," Mary laughed, slipping an arm under Bart's.

"I can see that," Bart chuckled.

"Belinda, do order me three more VIP passes and have them sent to my box, will you," Bart said to the ticket booth lady as they approached.

"But we can pay," Emma stammered.

"Not when you are with me," the dapper old man grinned, waving Emma's money away.

"You have a box?" Zoe inquired politely. "That's marvelous."

"Speaking of Marvelous, how do you think the colt will do today," Sylvie inquired, impressed by the deference the staff were giving Mary's new squeeze as they walked through the concourse. The sheer massiveness of the facilities filled with thousands of race fans was daunting.

"Do tell us, dear," Mary asked. "Did you get a chance to talk to his owner? Is he open to selling him?"

"I did ask him," Bart responded. "He said an equivocal 'We'll see'. It will indeed depend on how the colt performs today and if the track stewards detect any funny business. We're keeping a close eye on the jockey. Marvelous Marvin may surprise us with a win. His odds have settled at three to one."

"You seem to have a lot of inside information," Maggie noted, her eyes fixed on Bart.

"That's because Bart is the Chairman of the track committee," Mary chuckled. "Didn't I tell you that? I guess I must have forgotten."

"Cheeky devil," Zoe smirked, lightly elbowing her friend.

"You guys are too much," Dee laughed.

Sylvie instantly spotted the three men she had met the day before watching the parade of racehorses walk by inside the concourse on the way to the track.

"I think I'll go chat with my new buddies over there," Sylvie pointed.

"I'll go with you," Maggie offered.

"Oh, I was hoping you'd show us your new filly," Emma pouted. "You know, so I can gush about her to Sam, before he pops a gasket when another horse shows up unexpectedly at the ranch."

"Me too," Dee declared, raising a hand in the air.

"I'm just along for the ride," Terri beamed. "Wherever the girls go, I go, so long as Chairman Bart can wait until later to bless his tickets."

"Come up to the box with me first to get your passes, girls, and then you can go anywhere," Bart roared amused by the gaggle of women he found himself in the middle of.

"I'll go with Sylvie then and keep her out of trouble," Zoe offered.

"And who is going to keep you out of trouble," Sylvie retorted. "Oh, well, come on Agatha."

"Who is Agatha, I thought that was Zoe?" Bart asked Mary, confused.

"I'll explain it all in the box, dear," Mary acquiesced.

"Be careful," Maggie hissed, tilting her head sideways and fixing Sylvie with a pointed look.

"I will, mother," Sylvie quipped.

"Oh, do relax, Mags, embrace that bold confidence you showed us all last night," Zoe concurred.

Maggie scowled, her face darkening, before she flipped her hair in Zoe's face and stocked off after Bart and the other ladies.

"Do you think we broke her already," Zoe whispered to Sylvie as they headed towards the odds makers standing beside the rail looking down the oval to where the horses walked onto the racetrack. People stood shoulder deep watching the regal parade of horses and handlers. It was quite the spectacle.

"Not likely," Sylvie snickered. "Some days, I wish I had half of Maggie's strength."

"Strength and weakness are flip sides of the same coin," Zoe advised her. "I got that from a fortune cookie."

"You're taking this too seriously," Sylvie snorted. "Or is it you're jealous of Mary and her new beau? You don't really want another husband, do you?"

"Of course, I do. I'd like my next husband to be rugged like your Sam though," Zoe shrugged. "Bart is a good looking fellow, and maybe I wish I had met him first, but oddly he is a bit too smarmy for my liking. I want my next husband to look buff with his shirt off. He doesn't even have to be rich, just nice, charming, and good in bed."

"Tell me you aren't still in love with Tommy?" Sylvie stopped, confronting her friend.

Zoe's face took on a faraway look. Sylvie wasn't sure if the spry senior was thinking of her scared faced convict lover-slash-former-fiancé or if she had forgotten to take her medication that morning. Zoe's dementia had been under control for over a year, but every so often it reared its ugly head.

Not now, Sylvie prayed.

"I do believe that is Sean and Lacy Finnegan on the far side of the oval," Zoe declared, looking towards a sharply dressed bowlegged round-faced man wearing a grey felt fedora, a jeweled bleached blond cherub faced aging beauty queen at his side. The man in question was leaning across the rail berating a track official.

"Sylvie," the Tom Brady lookalike waved to her. "Over here."

"How's it hanging, you guys," Sylvie shouted over the din of the crowd, dragging Zoe along with her. "Got any hot tips for us old ladies?"

Tom Brady and his two compatriots greeted them warmly. Sylvie introduced them to Zoe.

"You're just in time for the first race," the stout peach colored redhead said to her. "I'm going with Strawberry Fields Forever. That's her over there."

"No, that filly's a hack, I'd go with Cash Him In," the brunette grinned.

"Strawberry Fields," Tom Brady agreed eyeing the strawberry roan with a white blaze, her gaze sweeping back and forth over the crowd as she walked by, a thin river of sweat running down her neck. "She's my pick."

"Strawberry Fields Forever it is," Sylvie laughed, glancing at Zoe.

An older jockey atop a gangly light bay with a white diamond on its forehead pranced by its eyes rolling in its head. The horse handler had a tight hold on the chain lead.

"That's the jockey," Zoe mouthed to her.

So, their two prime suspects, the Finnegan's and the jockey, were both here at once. If that wasn't a sign, nothing was.

"Who is that jockey aboard that light bay with the diamond?" Sylvie asked the men.

"That's the bugger that should be banned from the track," Tom Brady hissed. "We pointed him out yesterday. Guys like that give racing a bad name. I'm still not wholly convinced he didn't throw the derby."

Sean Finnegan shook his fist at the offending jockey. The jockey flipped the old man the bird and walked on.

"See what I mean," Brady scowled. "Guy's got no respect."

"So, where do I go to place a bet," Sylvie smiled sweetly, changing the subject.

"You can place it with me," the brunette said, flipping a small notepad open. Sylvie hadn't even noticed him holding one. "How much do you want to bet on Strawberry Fields? I can only give you 2 to 1 to win as she is the favorite. I don't do 'place' bets, only to win right now."

"How about two hundred dollars," Sylvie asked. "Is that enough? I can double that if you think I should?"

The men chuckled, their faces alight with glee.

"Two hundred is fine," the brunette said, writing her name and a figure in his book. "What's your full name, Sylvie?"

It was time, Sylvie thought. She turned to Zoe. Zoe nodded encouragement.

"O'Hara," she purred, pleased by the startled looks on the three bookies faces.

"Any relation to Cade O'Hara," the brunette asked, his scowl deepening.

"Yes, he was my husband," Sylvie sighed. "I buried him a few days ago. That's why I'm here. It's my way of celebrating his life, even if he was a scoundrel."

"Sorry for your loss," Tom Brady mumbled.

Redhead nodded agreement, his freckles seeming to darken.

Sylvie could see the men were now distinctly uncomfortable as they cast furtive glances her way.

"Oh, don't look so down," Sylvie laughed lightly. "We weren't on the best of terms when last we saw each other. As a matter of fact, I hadn't seen him in almost two years until I had to identify his body at the morgue."

"It was a dreadful experience," Zoe chimed in.

"Gosh that must have been horrible," Tom Brady agreed.

"Have they found out who did it yet?" the brunette asked, his eyes glittering.

"No, not yet," Sylvie pouted, dabbing a fake tear from her eye. "I doubt they ever will."

A horn sounded and the horses and their jockeys were led to the racetrack by the handlers. Strawberry Fields Forever was number three and the despised jockey on the light bay was number seven.

Sylvie caught movement across the way. Mrs Finnegan leaned into her husband, whispering something in his ear, her elaborate yellow derby hat flopping over one eye. Her expensive and overly large diamond and emerald necklace, earrings and bracelet glinted in the sunlight. Mrs Finnegan's clothing was just as expensive as her jewelry. Despite the designer clothing, the woman's stomach sagged, and she needed a plastic surgeon to fix the bad boob job. As one, the two turned to glare at Sylvie.

So, that was Cade's new main squeeze and her doting husband? Sylvie wasn't impressed, nor was she amused by the degree to which Sean Finnegan examined her.

"I heard on the news that your husband's winnings were never found," the brunette said, his shoulder pressing against hers. He was so close Sylvie could smell his Polo aftershave.

"That's true," Sylvie said overly loud. "About four hundred thousand appears to be unaccounted for, but the authorities are looking into it. I'm told there may have been a substantial fee paid to the man who cashed Cade's winnings. The tax department is on his ass."

"Interesting," the brunette said, breaking into a grin. "The tax man, you say."

"A man named Steele. He confronted me at the funeral, demanding I pay taxes on money I never saw and knew nothing about," Sylvie smirked. "Fellow takes his job rather seriously. I don't envy whoever helped Cade out, but then Cade had a way of leaving a path of destruction behind him, especially with the ladies."

"He did that," the brunette agreed.

"Oh, you knew my husband," Sylvie inquired, keeping her eyes on the television screen above their head, watching as the horses entered the gate.

"We all did," the bookie said. "Tell me, what did he go down for?"

"Huh?"

The bell rang and the horses were off. Sylvie switched her attention to the race, her mind reeling. Go down for what? Did he mean jail time? Cade never went to jail.

She and Zoe got caught up in the race, screaming out Strawberry Fields's name at the top of their lungs. The crowd watching the race on the screens erupted as the horses crossed the finish line. Strawberry Fields came in second. The supposedly crooked jockey on the bay came in fourth.

Sylvie turned back to the bookie. "You lose some, you win some," she shrugged.

"You are good for it, right?" he eyed her critically.

"I don't need Cade's winnings," she grinned. "Old money and all that. He had two nickels to rub together when we met, and he left with no more than the pajamas on his back. Now what was that about going down for something? I don't understand."

"Sorry. When I first met your husband, I guess it was about a year ago, he walked with a prison shuffle; you know head down, eyes downcast, shuffling gate. I assumed he just got out of the joint."

"My husband never went to jail, at least as far as I know," Sylvie replied, puzzled. "I'll ask the sheriff when I see him."

"You do that," the bookie nodded. "Care to pick a loser for the next race?"

Sylvie laughed delightedly. She wasn't as big a mark as he thought she was.

"Let's take a look at the horses first, shall we," she said, inclining her head towards the next set of horses being led into the concourse.

Lacy Finnegan shot daggers at her across the way, her once pretty face appearing grey beneath the pancake layer of makeup she wore. Sean Finnegan grabbed his wife roughly by the arm and dragged her off.

Sylvie caught Zoe's eye. They nodded at each other. Bart said his passes would get them in anywhere so they shouldn't need Maggie's help to get into the stables on race day or anywhere else.

"If you gents will excuse us for a few minutes, we're going to head to the loo and grab a drink to drown our sorrows. I'll catch you for the third race," Sylvie told the brunette.

"I know where to find you," the man's eyes twinkled. "It was all over the news. You looked delicious at the funeral by the way, and were those cowboy boots you made of point of showing to the tax collector up close and personal?"

"They were," Sylvie cooed, batting her eyes at him. "And don't worry, I always pay my debts, sweetie."

"I bet you do. If you ever want to have a fling with a younger man, just ask around for Johnny Brillio," he winked at her. "Everyone who is anyone knows me around here, plus I own a popular night club in Vegas, The After Eight. It's off the strip."

"Oh, come on, Johnny, not everyone knows you. You only show your face at the big races and only after one of your rubes wins big," Tom Brady kidded him.

Johnny Brillio shot Tom Brady a murderous look. Brady snapped his jaw shut and looked apologetic.

Interesting, Sylvie thought as she and Zoe turned their backs on the bookies and headed for the gate.

***

Maggie downright glowed as she showed off her new purchase to Emma, Dee and Terri.

"She's beautiful," Dee gushed rubbing the filly's velvet nose.

"I know," Maggie agreed. "Can you imagine what her foals are going to look like in a couple of years?"

"Foals? As in plural," Dee laughed.

"Definitely," Maggie beamed.

"Who are you going to breed her to," Emma asked. "Storm, Buddy or Zippo? Anyone of those studs would produce a magnificent foal with her."

"Babies, whoo hooo," Terri cried. "I can't wait either and I like my horses made of steel."

"I hadn't thought of Zippo, but you are right, he would produce a nice crossover as well," Maggie considered. "I haven't decided on whether to focus on producing a hunter quality horse which is usually larger boned or a jumper. Sadie told me that Shade loves to jump anything in the yard. If so, Storm would be the best choice."

"I guess you have to wait for her to mature though, huh," Emma nodded.

"At least a couple of years," Maggie conceded. "She's only two. Once she has a chance to mature and grow, we'll see what we have then. I thought I'd get BJ to work with her. He is doing such an amazing job with Expresso's ground manners. This little lady is broke for the track so I want to keep up her training, but I don't want to push too hard. She won't ever race again. What do you think about that, Emma?"

"You'll have a hard time keeping BJ away from her," Emma chuckled.

"That boy of yours is going to be a sought-after trainer one day, mark my words," Maggie smiled.

"Yes, I've been told," Emma beamed.

"Watch out," someone hollered as the jockey aboard a blood bay jumped off the rearing horse. The grooms leapt into the fray, one grabbing the bridle, while another slipped a lead line over the dancing horse's neck and held on tight until the colt settled down.

"Bloody nag, bagged out at the end as always," the jockey muttered angrily.

The colt shied away from him.

"That's the jockey we need to question," Maggie elbowed Emma.

"About what?" she asked, puzzled.

"About whether he threw the race that Cade won all the money on," Maggie seethed. "He might be our killer."

"Nasty piece of work isn't he," Dee snorted.

"Maybe he's just frustrated," Terri offered.

"Doubt that," Sadie hissed, coming up behind them. She wore red and silver colors, spit polished black boots, and a racing helmet. She tugged the racing helmet straps tight. "The horses hate him. He's a sod. It's too bad really; he was a great jockey once."

"Are you riding next," Emma ventured, liking the girl instantly.

Shade nuzzled Sadie's jacket. Sadie ruffled the horse's forelock and then planted a kiss on her nose.

"You must be Sadie, the illustrious jockey and trainer Maggie told us about," Dee laughed.

"One and the same," Sadie grinned. "Sorry, I can't chat, but I have to go weigh in. Bet on London Fog today in the Futurity. He's in great shape. I've got two other horses to ride before then though, so I won't see you again."

"Who are the others, we'll bet on all of them," Terri said enthusiastically.

"Oh, no, I'd get suspended for that," the jockey laughed.

They watched the tiny little waif in the colorful racing silks walk away. Almost every horse in the stable tried to say 'hello' to her when she passed. She had a kind word for all of them.

"She's amazing," Dee said. "Did you see the horses? They really do adore her. She's just like you described Maggie."

"Her they adore, yes, that other chap, no," Maggie snorted. "Look at him, waving his whip about. I'm going to go confront him. You girls stay here. You can come to my rescue if I need it, but only if I yell at you."

"Maggie, be careful," Dee warned.

"Dee's right. I don't want to preside over your funeral any time soon," Terri agreed.

"You are not going alone, I'm going with you," Emma blanched.

Maggie eyed her critically, Maggie's lip finally twitching upwards into a smile. Emma stood her ground. Her mouth went dry, and her legs trembled, but she wasn't going to back down. If her daughter could face down a mountain lion singing a Dolly Parton song, she could protect Maggie from a short guy thin as angel hair pasta.

Maggie marched briskly over to the man in the purple and magenta racing colors.

"You there," Maggie snapped. "I want to talk to you."

"I'm not interested in riding that filly," the jockey hissed. "I don't ride for the Nesbitt's or anyone dumb enough to buy a horse from them."

"That's not what I want your for," Maggie growled, straightening her six-foot frame. Though her hair was starting to turn white and age spots dotted the back of her hands, Maggie Carroll cut a commanding figure. She towered over the five-foot tall one-hundred-and-ten-pound jockey. Lesser men had crumbled under her intense scrutiny.

"What do you want then," he spat. "I've only got twenty minutes and then I have to head back to the weigh in room. I'm only here because of that damn colt, the knot head."

"I want to know if you knew Cade O'Hara?" Maggie thundered. "And don't lie to me or I'll throw you under the first stallion that walks by and cheer him on while he tramples you to death."

Emma took a step back. Maybe Maggie didn't need protecting after all.

"Yeah, I knew him," the jockey growled, stepping closer to the woman who glared fiercely at him. "Lower your damn voice."

"Fine, how's this?" Maggie replied sweetly, lowering her tone, and folding her arms over her chest.

"Who are you to him? Are you his wife?"

"What if I am," Maggie queried, leaning over him.

"Because he owes me money, that's why," the jockey muttered. "He owes me ten g's."

"What for," Maggie purred, changing tact.

"What do you think," the jockey hissed. "Wait a minute; you're from the club, aren't you? Trying to trip me up?"

"I am not from the club," Maggie grumbled. "I was Cade's mis…. friend. His wife's my best friend. I'm here on her behalf."

"Look," the jockey said, glancing around to make sure nobody could hear them. His eyes stopped on Emma. Emma discreetly backed up a few steps. "We had a deal. I was supposed to throw the derby at the last minute, but I didn't need to, see? Steam Train couldn't hack it. He hates the mud. That snot nosed uppity filly beat him fair and square. Cade, he flipped me the bird, said he didn't owe me anything."

Emma fought back a grin. After raising two kids, one of which was as strong willed as Maggie, she had developed stellar listening skills.

"So, you paid him back, didn't you," Maggie sneered. "You made sure he'd never snooker you again, followed him and put a bullet in his head."

"I did nothing of the sort," the jockey yelled, pushing away from her. "I've had my fill of guys like him, always wanting something, got some angle they're working on. They only care about themselves; couldn't care less about the damage they cause. I'm glad he's dead. That's all I'll say. Leave me alone, I got a job to do."

Maggie let the short angry man storm off.

"That went well," Emma grinned.

"You know I believe the leprechaun," Maggie scoffed. "He's an angry little man, but I don't think he's a killer."

"I pity the horse he rides next," Emma said.

"With any luck it will toss him at the gate," Maggie chuckled cruelly.

There was the Maggie Emma knew and loved – lurking beneath the surface.

***

It took some doing, but Sylvie and Zoe finally managed to get across the concourse and follow Sean and Lacy. If it wasn't for Lacy's immense hat, they'd have lost them in the ever-growing mass of race goers. They struggled to keep up to the couple as they passed the horses on the way to the warm-up enclosure down the sandy path leading to the stables. Sean was still red faced and irate. Lacy looked equally as angry. It was a long haul in the heat.

"Sylvie," Zoe stammered.

"Yes, Zoe," Sylvie replied, her eyes fixed upon the couple. Stable hands and grooms dodged the couple as if they had the plague. Even the jockeys on the way to the weigh in room avoided their eyes.

"I don't feel very well," her friend answered, rubbing her temple. "I'm quite dizzy."

"Maybe it's all the excitement."

"Could be," Zoe said, rubbing her temples harder.

"It could be dehydration as well," Sylvie offered, her heart breaking for the usually energetic woman at her side.

"You could be right," Zoe agreed, forcing a smile. "I'm sorry. I'm ruining everything for you. I don't think I can go on."

"No, you're not, ruining everything," Sylvie assured her, watching in disappointment as the two thoroughbred owners disappeared around the corner of the stable row. "Can you make it to Maggie's stall? She'll be there with the girls. They can get you some water."

"I can," Zoe nodded. "Just point me in the right direction."

"Are you sure," Sylvie asked, her brow creasing with worry. She was torn. She didn't want to leave Zoe unattended but didn't want to give up on her quest either. In truth, her own legs were shaking after the marathon walk.

Sylvie spotted a first aid attendant walking towards them carrying a can of Pepsi in one hand and a hotdog in the other.

"Excuse me," Sylvie called, waving the attendant over. "My friend is a little dizzy. I think it's the heat or maybe dehydration. Can you help her?"

"Of course, miss," the man said. "We've had a lot of that today. The heat's a killer."

Zoe smiled gratefully, her eyes narrow slits, as reeled sideways.

"Let me call a golf cart for you," the attendant said, dropping the half-eaten hotdog and calling for a golf cart on his walkie talkie.

"This fine young man will look after you," Sylvie reassured her friend. "Once you're feeling better, ask someone to take you to Bart's race box. I'll find you there. Are you okay if I leave you alone?"

"Go," Zoe quipped. "Promise me you'll get one of the girls to go with you though."

"Promise," Sylvie lied again.

She was getting rather good at that...lies. Lies, lies, and more lies, one on top of the other. It wasn't a good thing.

"Off with you then," Zoe commanded.

The attendant took Zoe by the arm, steadying her, as they waited for the first aid crew to arrive.

"My, you're rather handsome," Zoe said, flirting with the young attendant.

"Thank you," Sylvie said to the attendant. With a shake of her head, she raced to the spot where she had last seen the two murder suspects.

Anger and fear drove her forward, both in equal measures. She owed it to Cade to find out who killed him and why? Their marriage had endured too many hardships to count. He may have been a hound dog, but he was always there when she needed him. In her heart, Sylvie was glad she hadn't killed him in a fit of rage. Broken hearts could be repaired, but still hearts were forever. It was a blot on her soul.

The barns were quieter than Sylvie thought they would be as she strode past numerous empty stalls. She didn't know where she was. Maggie's new horse's stall was around here somewhere. Zoe was right about one thing – she shouldn't be doing this alone.

A blue sign pointed her towards the trailer parking and a loading/unloading zone. She assumed the couple had gone there, but why would they leave when they had two horses here, one in the Futurity race at the end of the day. She didn't know when the other horse ran. Still, it made no sense.

Sylvie's heart pounded in her chest. She struggled for breath, her age catching up to her. Her legs felt like jelly. What she wouldn't give to have her stallion beneath her now. Maybe she should have gone with Zoe to the first aid hut.

"Just a stubborn old fool, aren't you," she berated herself, grabbing a seat on a hay bale left leaning against a stall door. The stall at her back was empty, the top half open and the bottom half closed. She relished the smells of home: horse manure, sweat and hay. In the distance she heard the cries of children laughing in the fair grounds and the racing announcements. Race number three was about to start. Had she already been gone that long?

"You certainly are a stubborn fool," Sean Finnegan growled, slamming the stall door shut above her head.

Lacy Finnegan flanked her on the other side.

Where on earth had they come from?

"I saw your picture on the news," Lacy hissed.

"Apparently you weren't alone in that," Sylvie snorted.

"So, Mrs Cade O'Hara, why are you following us?" Sean barked, tapping her on the shoulder with a dressage whip.

Tap. Tap. Tap.

Sylvie grew annoyed. She looked up into the steely eyes regarding her with cruel interest. Two could play at that game. She glared back.

"I wanted to see what kind of man allowed his wife to be diddled by my lackluster husband," Sylvie chortled, driving the knife in. "Makes you a bit of a cuckold, doesn't it?"

"Witch," Lacy sneered. "At least I wasn't married to him."

"Hmmm, Cade had his virtues," Sylvie shrugged, meeting Lacy's gaze, "but you know all about those, don't you?"

Sean cracked the dressage whip across Sylvie's back. Sylvie shot straight up. Screaming, Sylvie round housed the horse trainer, punching him in the chin and then laying a fervent kick to the shins. He staggered backwards but recovered quickly. Lacy threw herself on top of Sylvie. Sylvie swung around in circles until the woman flew off, falling to the ground in a heap. She then hauled off and punched the woman in the face, her antique wedding ring shattering Lacy's nose. Lacy staggered off, squealing in pain, blood dripping out of her nostrils, her yellow hat flying off her head.

Sylvie grinned with satisfaction. That will teach the cheating hussy not to mess with another woman's husband.

Sean pushed Sylvie onto the hay bale, twisting her hands painfully behind her back, and scrunching her face sideways into the coarse hay. Sylvie choked as she inhaled the grassy pollen and mold. Her lungs constricted painfully. Her body and knees trembled.

That will teach me not to gloat, Sylvie grunted, fighting to stay conscious.

"I'm going to do you like I did your husband, silly woman," Sean fumed.

"Why?" Sylvie gasped, knowing she didn't have much time. "Why for God's sake?"

"Because he killed my older brother," Sean snarled. "I was only a teen at the time. My parents wouldn't let me go to the trial, but I remember his picture from the papers. I recognized him as soon as I saw him at the track."

"And you had your wife seduce him to get close to him," Sylvie croaked, hay lodging in her throat.

"I did," he sneered. "He was a chatty little bugger in the sack."

"That's all we need to hear, isn't it Cole?" Gus' calm voice echoed in Sylvie's ear as he wrestled Sean off Sylvie. Sylvie had never been so grateful in all her life to see the Law come to her rescue. "You're under arrest for the murder of Wallace O'Hara, Mr Finnegan."

"And you for accessory to murder, Mrs Finnegan," Cole replied, his voice equally as level, flipping his handcuffs around and around on one finger.

Sylvie sat up and coughed out a wad of grass and phlegm. It felt good to breathe again, but her arms were screaming with pain. "Who on earth is Wallace O'Hara," she asked, rubbing her throat. "And when did you two get here?"

Gus snapped the handcuffs on Sean while Cole grabbed hold of Lacy's arm, leaving her nose to continue to bleed.

Maggie, Emma, Dee and Terri raced around the far side of the barn. They came to a screeching halt at the sight of the Finnigans being arrested by Gus Rodriquez and Cole Trane.

At the same time, Mary and Zoe flew down the grounds towards them on a golf cart piloted by Mary's new beau, Bart, dust billowing out behind them.

"Wallace, aka Wally O'Hara was Cade's brother. He was using Cade's name because he was banned from racetracks all over North America because he confessed to the murder of one Danny Finnegan, professional jockey, after Mr Finnegan decided not to throw a race that he was paid to do by the mob. Wally went to jail for a crime he didn't commit to save his own skin," Gus explained as Dee and his sister rushed to his side.

"He was jailed with Tommy wasn't he," Mary boomed. "I saw him. Remember the day we got kidnapped Sylvie? I thought I saw Cade in the yard... or was it you who saw him and told me? I can't quite remember."

"I thought I saw him too," Zoe agreed.

"So, who did I bury then?" Sylvie demanded, looking from Gus to Cole. "And where's the money?"

"You buried Wally," Cole sighed. "We found Cade yesterday."

"Where was he, the so and so?" Maggie hissed, wrapping a protective arm around Sylvie.

"Somehow his body must have ended up in the manure pile at the ranch," Gus continued, "and it was taken away and turned into compost."

"Yuck," Zoe grinned. "That's morbid."

"Not really, they're starting to talk about a composting option for people now," Terri replied nonchalantly.

"You mean I killed the wrong man," Sean raged.

"And I slept with that ugly prune for no reason," Lacy sobbed.

"Probably not the first time," Mary quipped.

"You killed the man everyone thought killed your brother," Gus said to Sean.

"Which was the wrong man anyway because he was using Cade's name," Maggie replied, mildly amused.

"Then who did kill my brother," Finnegan asked quietly.

"Harry the Hammer, a bookie and loan shark from Boston," Gus informed him. "He confessed to the murder in exchange for witness protection and his testimony against two crime families we've been trying to take down for years."

"So, you're saying I did kill Cade then," Sylvie muttered, slumping against Maggie.

"You did, Sylvie," Cole groaned. "I have to arrest you."

"Cole… not now," Emma sobbed.

"I'm sorry, Em, it's my job," Cole sighed.

"Does Sam know," Sylvie whispered hoarsely.

"Not yet," Cole nodded. "I'll let you tell him when we get back."

"Thank you for that," Sylvie murmured.

"You're not handcuffed yet," Mary yelled, pushing Bart from the golf cart. "We can make a run for it!"

"Yes, let's." Zoe cried, reaching out a hand for Sylvie to jump in beside her.

"I've got your back," Maggie screamed, racing for a metal pitchfork and holding it up like a lance, swinging it back and forth between Gus and Cole.

The men reached for their guns.

Emma, Dee and Terri jumped in the way, effectively barricading off the golf cart.

Sylvie snorted back the tears. She held up her hands to the girls, signaling them to all stand down. "No," she said stubbornly. "It's time to face the music. I need to pay for my crime."

"But we were going to buy a racehorse today," Zoe sulked. "I'd like to own a racehorse still. Maggie can't be the only one to own a racehorse."

"And it is Razzle Dazzle Me in the lead, Chocolate Sauce in second, Leyland in third, and here comes Marvelous Marvin on the outside," the announcer screamed over the sound system.

"Marvelous Marvin is my horse," Sean started, straightening up despite the handcuffed arms behind his back.

"It's Razzle Dazzle Me and Marvelous Marvin."

"Stop, we don't want Marvin to win, we want to buy him," Zoe yelled.

"It's Marvelous Marvin for the win," the announcer yelled.

"That's funny, Miguel told me not to bet on him," Zoe sobbed. "I was going to, but he said the jockey was 'iffy'."

"Oh, we replaced the jockey minutes before the race. He and Sean had a row. You can still buy the colt," Lacy smirked. "Marvelous Marvin is registered to me. All of the horses are registered to me, and I need a good lawyer."

"LACY!" Sean yelled.

Lacy shrugged.

"But what happened to Cade's…er, Wally's winnings?" Sylvie asked mildly. "You can't have spent all of it, surely?"

"Racehorses cost a fortune to train and maintain," Sean grumbled. "Not to mention my wife has expensive tastes."

"Don't worry, we'll relieve her of those," Cole chuckled.

Sylvie, Maggie, Zoe and Mary grinned.

"Well, that will give me something to chat with the girls in the yard about," Sylvie shrugged.

"You'll be famous," Maggie chuckled.

"Just like me and Mags," Zoe agreed.

"I heard you also own London Fog," Mary asked Lacy innocently. "Perhaps we can make a deal before the bailiffs get to him."

Chapter Twenty-One

Whinnying in everything

The ranch was decorated with white and red carnations. Lady's breath and green ivy garlands were wrapped around the porch columns. Strands of white icicle lights hung from the porch and the top of a huge white open sided circus tent in the yard. A rose arbor stood at the front of the tent. The tables inside the tent were topped with crisp white table clothes with dusty rose-colored candles and green ivy centerpieces. A rearing stallion ice sculpture graced the head table. The head table itself was a longer than usual affair.

The mountain in the distance was ringed with Fall color. Gold, orange and red leaves created a brilliant back drop against the golden fields dotted with Black Angus cattle. The sky was blue with bits of fluffy white clouds rolling about as if they were Mother Nature's after thought.

One burro, a mule, a one eared donkey, a handful of ranch horses, and a bay colt watched the proceedings from their pens. The DNA results had come in. The colt's father wasn't the white, red or bay stallions. As it turned out, the old paint stallion wasn't done yet. The electric fence in his paddock now stood a foot taller than all the rest.

A sea of men dressed in cowboy boots, black jeans and suit jackets, white shirts with bolero ties, and women in fancy boots and frilly lace dresses lined the bride's walk from the barn to the front porch where Pastor Terri Scallon stood in her very best vestments. The two Saint Bernards, Bulldozer and Dozer Junior, lay on either side of her, freshly bathed for the day's events. Gus and Cole in black tuxedoes flanked the pastor.

Jenny Montana rode her red and white roan appaloosa pony into the yard. She wore a frilly pink flower girl dress. Her flaming curls were the same color as the pony's chest. Pink ribbons adorned her pony's mane and tail. Jenny's cheeks were flushed with pleasure. BJ rode behind her on Maggie's black thoroughbred filly. The filly also sported pink ribbons in her mane and tail. BJ looked sharp in knee high dressage riding boots and a black top hat, coat and tails with grey breeches.

The crowd held their breath as Sam rode Zoe's mare out next, his stained Stetson replaced by a new black felt hat with a red hawk feather in the brim. He wore a black coat and tails with an ivory shirt underneath, his prized reining gold belt buckle, and his worn cowboy boots peeked out from under his freshly ironed black jeans. There were some things that Sam Montana wouldn't change for anyone. The white Andalusian pranced beneath him, nostrils flared, its steps slow and elegant as it danced harmoniously down the aisle to the wedding march.

The wedding party let out a collected sigh as Emma, Sylvie, and Dee rode three dark bay horses side-by-side across the yard, Sylvie's stallion in the middle, looking fiercely elegant between the little mustang and Quarter horse. Sylvie wore an ivory Spanish lace wedding dresses, the other two ladies were pure white, each dress having miniature differences at the waist and collars, but all complementing the other, long trains falling over the horse's rumps in a tidal wave of lace.

Jenny and BJ sidestepped their horses to one side as Sam reined up in front of Terri. He dismounted the mare, handing the horse off to one of Cole's deputies. Sam climbed the steps and took his place beside Cole and Gus.

"We are gathered here today to join Gus and Dee, Emma and Cole, and Sam and Sylvie, in holy matrimony," Terri said, her face breaking into an award-winning smile. "Gentlemen, take your places beside your brides please."

The men elbowed each other good naturedly and stepped down off the porch, each of them walking over to stand beside their prospective brides who were still mounted on their steeds.

"And who is here to give Emma's hand away in marriage," Terri shouted to be heard over the murmurs of approval filling the air.

"I am," BJ yelled.

The wedding party cheered.

"And who is here to give Dee's hand away in marriage," Terri asked again.

"I am," Dee's father announced proudly stepping out of the crowd.

"And who is here to give away Sylvie's hand away in marriage," Terri finished.

"We are," Mary, Zoe, and Maggie shouted, galloping into the yard on their stallions in an array of brown and white, white, and red. The stallions snorted and arched their necks, swishing their tails, each trying to outperform the other.

The ladies arranged the stallions behind the brides' horses.

"This is just in case one of you decides to change your mind," Mary shouted. "You aren't getting past any of us."

A raucous cheer went up.

"Not likely," Sylvie joked, glancing down at Sam.

Terri laughed and continued the ceremony much to the delight of everyone including the horses.

"And now for the rings," Terri said, nodding at Jenny.

Jenny trotted her pony up to Gus, Cole and her grandfather, handing each of them a differently colored ring box.

"I think I'm supposed to have the red one," Gus whispered to Sam.

"Yeah, and the blue one's mine," Cole said.

The men swiftly exchanged jewelry boxes.

"Slip the rings on their fingers, gents. I now pronounce you men and wives," Terri hollered gleefully. "You may kiss the brides… or bride, just one, your bride, not all of them."

The crowd laughed heartily as the men swept their brides off their horses and into their arms.

Gus and Dee kissed passionately, and then Cole and Emma matched them, each man trying to outperform the other, refusing to end the kiss. The wedding party clapped and cheered.

"Let me show y'all how it's done," Sam smirked, lifting Sylvie from the stallion's back.

The prison monitoring bracelet around Sylvie's ankle got caught in the stirrup leathers. She clung to Sam, one foot in the air, her dress sliding up so that everyone could see the blue garter circling her thigh and the sexy black silk underwear beneath her gown.

"Something borrowed, something blue," Sylvie laughed.

"A little help here," Sam chuckled, nodding to a second deputy standing on the other side of the wedding party. The deputy raced over and unhooked the ankle bracelet.

"Don't set that off," Sylvie joked. "We don't have enough food for the State troopers too."

"Isn't it nice to know the law is here to help us out in a crisis," Sam whispered in Sylvie's ear, before planting Sylvie's feet on the ground, whipping off his hat, and bending Sylvie over backwards to illustrate to the young men in the crowd how a real man shows his love.

Not to be outdone by some old cowboy, the two lawmen followed suit.

The End

I hope you enjoyed the final installment in *The Silver Spurs Series*. Please don't forget to leave a review on [Amazon](), [Bookbub]() or [Goodreads]() or any other of your own social media pages. It truly means a lot to authors and their families and publishers.

While this series has come to an end, do check out Laura on [Amazon](). There is something for readers of all ages and in various genres.

If you want to hear about upcoming releases, then visit Laura's [website/blog]() and hit the "Follow Me" button or follow Laura on [Goodreads]() or [Bookbub]().

Acknowledgements

A special thanks to my friends, Dee Gallant, the 'Cougar Whisperer' from Vancouver Island, and Terri Scallon, who agreed to let me do anything with their characters, and to Deb Nicol for being my sounding board for this crazy trio of madcap western mystery novels.

And of course, a heart felt thank you to the readers who joined me in this adventure.

Other Books by Laura Hesse

The Holiday Series (family adventure):

One Frosty Christmas, The Great Pumpkin Ride, A Filly Called Easter, Independence and Valentino

Paranormal Thriller:

The Thin Line of Reason

The Gumboot & Gumshoe Series:

Book One: *Gumboots, Gumshoes & Murder*
Book Two: *The Dastardly Mr. Deeds*
Book Three: *Murder Most Fowl*
Book Four: *Gertrude & The Sorcerer's Gold*
Book Five: *Chasing Santa*

The Silver Spurs Series

The Silver Spurs Home for Aging Cowgirls
Bandits, Broads & Dirty Dawgs
Who Killed Cade

Paranormal Fantasy:

Lucifer and Mary Jane: All The Devil's Horses

Comedy & Adventure:

Peter Pan Wears Steel Toes

If you want to find hear about her upcoming releases, then visit her website at www.RunningLProductions.com.

About the Author

Laura lives on Vancouver Island with a rescue dog and two old cats. She grew up a back stage brat in Music Hall Theatre and credits her mother with her love of the Arts. She loves to sing at local jams when she can.

Laura spent many happy years riding the trails and writes about the special horses in her life within the pages of her children's and young adult series of equine novels. While Sally and all the rest have passed over the rainbow, they will forever live on in her stories.

Peace and wellness to all.

Made in the USA
Las Vegas, NV
02 June 2022